Journeying
to the Light

Daily Readings through
Advent and Christmas

John Mann

Published by Messenger Publications, 2023

Royalties from this book will be donated to the St German's
Cathedral Foundation for Music and the Arts.

ISBN: 9781788126465

Designed by Brendan McCarthy
Typeset in Garamond Premier Pro and Cormorant Garamond
Printed by Hussar Books

Messenger Publications,
37 Leeson Place, Dublin D02 E5V0
www.messenger.ie

Contents

Preface by Bishop Brendan Leahy...v

Introduction.. 1

First Week of Advent.. 3

Second Week of Advent.. 19

Third Week of Advent.. 37

Fourth Week of Advent 57

Christmas... 75

Acknowledgements

This book appears only as a result of the encouragement and help of a number of people, some of whom are almost certainly unaware that their words have been a source of support and direction. More specifically, my wife Helen, and our family, have continually spurred me on, and Kay Firth in proof-reading and with grammatical suggestions has been invaluable. Richard Ryan, of *The Book Well*, and Michael Brennan have been very helpful too. The advice, support and encouragement of Cecilia West and all at Messenger Publications, and the kind commendations of several bishops, have made everything towards the final production smooth and straightforward, and brought these thoughts on Advent and Christmas to a happy conclusion. I am extremely grateful to you all!

John Mann

Preface by Bishop Brendan Leahy

I am delighted to write this preface to a book that is such a wonderful Advent-Christmas gift. I do so not least because I have enjoyed many years of ecumenical friendship with the author, John Mann, for which I am most grateful.

We know how easily we can skim the surface of these days and weeks. Yes, we have Advent calendars and, of course, many of us will hear the Carols and attend Nativity plays, but there's not much in the way of a sustained daily reflection to accompany us. That's where this book is so valuable. In these short daily comments, almost like diary entries, John weaves together mature insights into Scripture, especially the prophet Isaiah, with personal observations on our everyday world, all the while lifting up our spirits.

John is a realist. Not everyone finds the five or six weeks of Advent – Christmas easy. These are busy weeks. And, on a deeper level, we know that vulnerability and strife, chaos and confusion are so much part of our personal and society's experience. What comes across again and again in this book, however, is John's conviction that the 'miracle of the Incarnation' has something very deep to say to us: God has come down to us and dwells with us. We have not been left abandoned or alone in life. God is close, God is involved in our lives and God is always new. Even the unexpected twists and turns all fit, in some mysterious way, into God's loving plan.

Each author, if he or she is authentic, reveals something of his or her own life experience. John offers many wonderful vignettes of his own life, not to focus on himself but rather to evoke in us memories of Christmases past and then too to make the links between the light of hope and our everyday lives. We hear of John's childhood in St Andrew's Hornchurch in Essex, his schools days in Blackheath, his various parish and cathedral appoints such as those in Swanage and Salisbury, and most especially of his significant service as Dean of Belfast Cathedral. I particular enjoyed reading on Day 21 one of John's first school reports declaring, in careful copperplate hand-writing, 'John has settled down into an habitual "old stager"… In the main he is rather quiet, but there is a riotous side to him which is well worth watching. He knows his own mind."

As an accomplished violinist, John has a musician's heart, attentive to the subtle tones of life's emotions and reactions. He notices and names what we can simply take for granted. The habitual is ruffled and the newness of what Advent and Christmas offer us are presented to us in their various aspects. The constant returning to the source of his med-itations in Scripture is admirable. We meet and learn from great bibli-cal figures such as Isaiah, Elijah, Micah, Zephaniah, John the Baptist, the Virgin Mary, with Christ a central focus throughout.

John helps us see how everyday life can become a launching pad for reflection. There's a homeliness, for instance, of reference in Day 11 to 'the moment in December when the dates go into double fig-ures, i.e. when we reach the tenth day of the month. This has always seemed like a tipping point for my wife and me. Usually one of us says, "Well, not long now and so much to do"' and so begins another phase of Advent. On Day 30 the theme of journey is brought out in a meditation that presents us with a Luas journey in Dublin taking in St Stephen's Green, Ranelagh and Harcourt Street. On Day 28 by recalling the Christmas nights of his childhood, John invites us to recall our own memories: 'what lives to this day is a sense that, on this night above all nights, we had been part of a thin – wafer thin – brush with eternity; shared across the ages of human life and held in the heart of God'.

The book is written against the canvas of our times with its many challenges. John gently but clearly reminds us that Advent and Christ-mas call us to personal and societal transformation. In the text for Day 9 he points out clearly: 'we are in control of our own resources and can help create the vision of Isaiah in lands that have millions of people living without hope'.

There are many gems in this text. Writing about the tradition of visiting people during Christmas, as he reflects on the meeting of Mary and Elizabeth, on Day 25, John offers kind advice: 'As we knock on the door, or ring the bell, with maybe a present or greeting card to hand, perhaps we could spare a thought for this meeting of Mary and Elizabeth; the absence of jealousy; the genuine joy of playing some part together in the mystery of God's amazing plan; the chance to share, with a smile and excitement and, yes, a blessing, with someone else whose life at that moment is crossing ours.' John offers wonderful commentaries on the Advent antiphons or refrains that mark liturgically the seven days before Christmas. He writes of John the Baptist: 'What everyone who listens to John the Baptist receives is hope'. In leading us in a journey into Light, through this book John guides us along the pathways of hope that are Advent and Christmas.

Bishop of Limerick,
Brendan Leahy

Prayer for use before the daily readings:
Heavenly Father,
Guide my thoughts,
Forgive my distractions,
Help me to listen to your Word,
In Jesus name.
Amen.

Prayer for use after the daily readings:
Loving Lord,
Help me to live this day,
Consecrated to you,
Seeking to serve,
Open to your Spirit,
Conscious of your love.
Amen.

Introduction

Advent, Christmas and Epiphany begin the Christian year and promote wonder, joy, hope and light. They have aspects that are dark, but this opening of the year for the Church is essentially positive. Not everyone will find these five or six weeks easy, for they coincide with the depth of winter and may bring back sad memories for some. The message that the Light of the World is coming, has arrived and is shown forth to all will bring the most down hearted the truth that in the birth of the Christ-child the miracle of the Incarnation is real. God has come down to us and dwells with us.

Where do we go for the inspiration to make a meaningful and devotional Advent and Christmas? Surely it is to the Scriptures, for their timeless words to speak once more into our hearts of the love of God. We will be helped in threading the way through the history of the children of Israel to the stable in Bethlehem by reading the words of the prophets and the gospel writers. We will see, once again, why it is that Emmanuel – God-with-us – transforms hearts and minds and lives.

Advent always begins on a Sunday, but its length and ending depends upon which day of the week Christmas Day falls. If it is a Monday, then Advent is just over three weeks, but if it is a Sunday as it was in 2022, then it is a full four weeks. Advent calendars get around this problem by not differentiating Sundays and simply beginning on 1 December, though in any one year that may not be the actual beginning of Advent or a Sunday.

Between Christmas and Epiphany there are either one or two Sundays, depending on the day of the week of Christmas Day itself. St Stephen's day, and those of St John the Evangelist and the Holy Innocents (normally 26, 27 and 28 December) can be transferred, if they fall on a Sunday, on to the nearest weekday following. This has led me to produce a schedule of readings with flexibility, in order that they can be used any year, rather than just in the year they are published. There are enough days for use in Advent in this book to allow for a full four weeks, so some can be omitted towards Christmas Eve when not required. Equally, I have treated the days after Christmas Day according to the dates, ignoring where the Sundays fall.

This appears to be a good place to mention the ecumenical nature of this book. There are Church traditions that all of us take for granted, yet may not be shared with other strands of the Christian Church. I write as an Anglican, of which Communion there is sufficient variation to require a glossary of terms alone, but chiefly I apologise to those of my many friends in the Roman Catholic Church, and in the Protestant Churches, if I have inadvertently either taken for granted something which I should have explained, or much worse, have caused offence in any of my words.

Many of the readings coincide with the daily Eucharist readings from the Revised Common Lectionary. I haven't been slavish to this schedule, but on most days before Christmas I have chosen a reading from the prophet Isaiah or the Gospel according to Luke. After Christmas the readings vary significantly for St Stephen, St John the Evangelist and the Holy Innocents (introducing Acts, John and Matthew), but, for the most part there are a mix of readings in the twelve days of Christmas, until we turn to Matthew for the coming of the Magi.

The prophecy of Isaiah is a natural accompaniment to the season of Advent. There is judgement pronounced on God's people from the 'Holy One of Israel', as the prophet declares Yahweh to be. Isaiah presents themes of the nation's blindness and deafness, describing the failures that are leading the people to ruin and exile. Isaiah's vision of restoration, fulfilment and promise is also presented with many glorious pictures of the transformed life to come.

Luke's Gospel needs no introduction. It holds one of only two accounts of the Nativity of our Lord in the Scriptures – the other being in Matthew. Luke's account is from Mary's perspective, Matthew's from Joseph's. Both are full of anticipation and wonder. There is no better place for us to begin.

2

FIRST WEEK OF ADVENT

Day 1

The First Sunday of Advent

'Therefore he shall give them up until the time when she who is
in labour has brought forth ...'
Today's reading: Micah 5:2–4

I launch us into our journey through Advent with the words of Micah.
They give us a jolt today. Through his prophet, Yahweh seems to be
saying that his people are abandoned until they are saved through a
new birth. Abandonment leaves people gutted and alone. Maybe
God's people just *felt* abandoned, or unable to improve their lot, but
however it was, they were about to be surprised by a miracle the circumstances of which continue to astonish us today. There is something about the birth of a baby that gives hope, and simply lifts
everyone, but this was to be a most unusual birth in very special
circumstances.

Sometimes we need a jolt in order to see things in a bigger way. I
am drawn to the words of Sr Agnes, an Anglican nun who lived a
solitary life on the Shetland isle of Fetlar. In *A Tide that Sings*, she
writes of this time of year, 'It was the season of Advent, full, like one's
childhood, of that joyful expectancy and clear apprehension of a life
evermore.' She seems to suggest that a process of peeling away what
we gather around us is going to help. Maybe this is what Micah is
getting at? Feeling abandoned could be described as sensing the loss
of protection. How often, I wonder, did the children of Israel know

5

themselves to be extremely vulnerable – just like a child? The child brings hope; the child brings anxiety too.

The gospel reading we will hear in church today, whether from Matthew, Mark or Luke, will give us Christ's intense warning of what is to come. This apocalyptic vision of a world collapsing into chaos is not something we wish to contemplate. It seems that it is always true that some part of our world is engulfed in strife. Throughout the ages, many people have seen in that strife a sign of closeness to the end-time. So often the vision of the world is one of disunity and discord. Such is woven into the psyche of the Christian who seeks, through prayer and penitence, to prepare in expectation for the coming of the Saviour. Abandonment to hope and abandonment to risk, or, as Sr Agnes puts it, joyful expectancy, attunes us; it awakens us to a clear apprehension of what eternal life means.

Day 2

Monday

'Nation shall not lift up sword against nation'
Today's reading: Isaiah 2:1–5

At the beginning of this Advent journey, we consider the state of the world into which Jesus was born. It was a world not unfamiliar to us in the twenty-first century: a place and time of hopes and dreams but also of division, conflict and brutality. People were drawn to Jerusalem, as in Isaiah's vision. They sought to recreate the pristine perfection of God's true intention: a place where human beings could live in peace and harmony.

Even today, people are drawn to Jerusalem. There is a profound and telling paradox in the search for unity in the city of Jerusalem, which is itself so deeply divided; as profound and telling as is the contemplation of the peace, forgiveness and reconciliation that was won for us on Calvary by Christ in the act of extreme violence and incomprehensible abuse of love that was the crucifixion. Walking the streets of the old city of Jerusalem today, one encounters the places of worship for Christians, Muslims and Jews within a few hundred metres of each other. They are each in their own way statements of the concentrated spiritual intent of each religious tradition. They are not only impressive, they are a clear indication of the strength of purpose that is declared in the practice of prayer.

It could seem chaotic. It is both moving and heart-breaking that men and women find their spiritual focus in such different ways. The situation is greatly different from that of the time of Christ. In the time of Christ the Temple dominated the city. People were drawn to it, but there was a sense that not everything was quite right. John the Baptist and Jesus were to reveal just where the cracks lay.

All these years later, we can start out towards Bethlehem knowing that our hearts and minds will be drawn to a place that reveals the vulnerable time in which we live and the critical situation of many millions of people. We need to recognise and own within ourselves this stark truth in a clear and analytical way. As we enter one of the busiest few weeks of the year, we shall try and tread the path to the birthplace of the Christ-child. We do this not in a state of illusion, believing that we are stronger than we are, perhaps even confident that we can put things right by the wielding of a sword, whilst, in fact, we cannot even handle the burden of a ploughshare.

Having learnt this, critically and with our eyes open, we can walk on praying that the Holy Spirit will guide us from the inner chaos and anxiety that is the place from which most people try and seek the face of God. Through this we gain the recognition that Christ is calling us to the stable as others have been led there before us. Let us take hope and joy in the vision before us today that has been held by Christians for more than two thousand years.

Day 3

Tuesday

'The Spirit of the Lord shall rest on him.'
Today's reading: Isaiah 11:1–10

Although I have spent most of my life in urban areas, that is not how I expected it to be. When I was ordained, I anticipated a life of rural ministry, but things did not work out that way.

Things do not always work out the way we picture them. As Christians, we interpret this within the providence of God and seeks to follow where we believe Christ leads. I would add to that a belief that where we take steps that are found later to have been clearly wrong our Lord can and does call us from there into a new place. Such is his love for us that, no matter what, it never fails. Somehow life with Christ demonstrates this; redirection, when it comes, though we may think of it like the recalibration of a sat-nav, is more akin to a friend walking with us, sometimes gently guiding and occasionally bringing us up sharply to see our error.

I recall some years ago, when I was in a rural parish, being interviewed by a researcher who was studying the reasons why people moved to the country. It was a beautiful, sunny, summer day, and we were sitting in the rectory garden overlooking the fields. I looked at him, and I just know that I had an expression on my face that read, 'Why do you need to ask?' But this man was an academic and genuinely interested in his subject, so, pityingly, he led me to take his question a bit more seriously. In fact his response taught me more about escapism than many a sermon that pleads with complacent Christian people to consider justice, reconciliation, poverty, and all the perils and evils of this world that may be righted if people will step up and be counted.

We got to talking about 'crying peace when there is no peace' and of hidden voices and of the struggle at the heart of God's creation. Well, this man was not there to talk of Christianity, or any other religious outlook upon the world, so let's just say we dwelt on the common concerns of humanity. I wonder what he would have made of the prophecy of Isaiah and especially of the words of the reading today from Chapter 11. These verses are familiar as one of the traditional Christmas Carol service readings and are loved by those who hear them, for they capture one of the great themes of Advent and give us hope.

Isaiah was looking to the future of Israel, but the Christian sees this in Christ. His birth is an actual fulfilment of this prophecy. His life is one where the Spirit of God is manifest constantly in transformation. Yesterday we dwelt on the chaos of the world fallen into sin and a vision of a world without war, today the restoration is further proclaimed by the coming of one from the line of Jesse, the father of King David.

It is a reading full of attractive images: the child leading the wild animals, the lion with the ox, the bear with the cow are feeding together, the holy mountain shall stand serene in its permanence, the universal accord with the God-ward inclination of humanity making the source of life the centre of everything forever. But reading these words is not escapism for Christians, as we see that these things have not been literally fulfilled in the coming of Jesus. So where do we sit with them? The world as pictured by Isaiah in these verses is one that, from the day of Christ's appearing, is part of the understanding that we have of the kingdom of God already present in our hearts, one day to be revealed in power and glory and majesty for all, as God's creation is transformed and consummated.

Day 4

Wednesday

'See, this is our God; we have waited for him,
so that he might save us.'
Today's reading: Isaiah 25: 6-10a

The fourth day of Advent, and I am usually ready to declare at this point, 'Is any of this Advent preparation worth it?' Day four, maybe even day three, of many an endeavour requiring discipline is so often when resolve fails. I have preached on this, written about it, and found from others that in busy lives things slip between the third and fourth day, and either I reset the task or give it up. It lifts my heart to acknowledge this as something normal. I realise that I am not alone in lacking an iron will and need more than a 'no pain, no gain' outlook in seeing the worth of preparing carefully for Christmas.

In taking my violin out of its case and turning up a piece of music, I look for something that will get my fingers and bowing arm moving but has a tune as well. A familiar but tuneful exercise is generally the starting point, or maybe straight into Bach. What do I find but that the minutes pass and what was an attempt to physically move myself becomes a satisfying inner pleasure. Something has brought me subconsciously and tangentially to a point that I wanted to reach but for which I wasn't aiming. Can our devotion be found this way as well?

The heart is the seat of both deception and paradox; do we not know this from our experience of life as much as from the Scriptures? It is also the source of craving, and that inner ache that can show itself in tears of sorrow as readily as through the volcanic chemistry of love. Isaiah expresses in his prophecy, in the verses that are chosen for today, the covering of the peoples of the world and the veil that is spread over the nations. The prophet is leading us to consider the revealing of what is hidden. Isaiah was considering the idea of a nation cast into the gloom of reproach and intimidation. In our own day, we can see peoples and countries enduring great anguish almost every time we turn on the news. Nothing in one sense changes as we think about what Isaiah is saying to us, but can we see that the light that Isaiah is lifting to our eyes is an inner light? It is one that cannot be quenched in the outer darkness, but, and herein lies part of our challenge, as we pray for those struggling in the dark places of this world, are we also able to embrace the corresponding inner darkness within which those who dwell there exist, whilst they, like us, are seeking to truly live?

Thomas Merton wrote of offering our own sins and sorrows and all our struggling with interior conflict to God, not in our own words, but through what he described as the 'action' of the psalms. On this day the appointed psalm for Holy Communion is Psalm 23. This is such a good starting point for entering this 'action' with an expression of inner fears, stepping courageously knowing the love of God, not being alone in that place of reassurance, but with those others who are equally troubled, confused and in need.

We can hold Advent without any difficulty because its vitality is internal, urgent, powerful. We will brush against Christmas as a spacecraft encounters the atmosphere of the earth before entering it, but the anticipation will not be lost if we rest there, knowing what is to come whilst pondering the reasons for the coming of the Saviour and devoting ourselves to the days of devotion and intercession that acknowledge a world in need of the true light to pierce the spreading veil of spiritual night.

Day 5

Thursday

'... the feet of the poor, the steps of the needy.'
Today's reading: Isaiah 26:1–6

The path of the distressed, of the fleeing refugee, the scarred victim of violence, the abused and the dazed, the mentally and physically shattered, is one we are only too familiar with, albeit not necessarily from personal experience. Though there is good reason to suppose that someone reading these words may have first-hand knowledge of what is a common enough occurrence both at home and abroad. The feet of the poor, the steps of the needy, have traversed the pages of novels, walked with the poets, fled starvation and disease millions of times more than we have seen them on camera, and Isaiah and other Old Testament writers have reminded the people of their responsibility to the outcast and stranger, the poor and the needy.

Now, in a hymn on the fall of worldly power and the lifting up of the downtrodden, Isaiah assists our Advent thoughts with the place of poor and needy in the new order that the coming of Jesus will usher in. It is possible that we may miss that bit at the end of what is in the *Irish Book of Common Prayer* a canticle entitled '*Urbs Fortitudinis*'. The lovers of matins amongst us will have sung verses 1–6 of chapter 26 many times, probably with the thought of the 'strong city', the place of the righteous nation, that will be kept in perfect peace and trusting in the Lord, the everlasting rock. But this, we recall, is the place of the meek of the earth. Jesus will later speak of this in the Sermon on the Mount, especially in the Beatitudes.

As we take a further step towards Christmas, let us think a little today of the poverty into which Jesus was born and the insecurity in which the Holy Family existed for some time after his birth. Isaiah is foreseeing a day when the powerless of the earth will walk where once the powerful held sway, and there will be no sign of the previous habitation for the dust is all that remains. The prophet is particularly poetic in the way he emphasises height and lowliness in his descriptions. The lofty city will be laid low to the ground.

Humanity has a short memory and imagines that the unassailable of today will remain in the ascendancy forever, but history shows that the only true and everlasting rock is that of the Lord. The Christian, in seeking to understand the coming of Messiah, is receiving images from a Hebrew faith community that held the vision of a world of justice and peace. Christ owned those images, and we have received the legacy of the kingdom founded upon the principles that he showed and taught from the day on his birth, and to which we continue to be drawn.

Day 6

Friday

'On that day the deaf shall hear the words of a scroll, and freed
from gloom and darkness the eyes of the blind shall see.'
Today's reading: Isaiah 29:17–24

The building of the transformed society that yesterday included the
poor and needy stepping through the dust of the proud empires of
the powerful now touches the lives of the deaf, who will hear words
read, and the blind, from whom gloom and darkness will be banished.

This has been a week through which we have been holding the
importance of Advent without mentioning the Advent antiphons,
John the Baptist and the Blessed Virgin Mary. We have only briefly
touched on matters such as creation, and sin, and light, that will begin
to occupy us more fully soon. We are rather dwelling on the vision
of the nature of the transformation of the world, linked to the coming of the Saviour, which is eagerly anticipated as Isaiah poetically
and prophetically declares it to be.

We are entering the darkest days of the year. Two weeks from now
we will encounter the shortest day, the old Feast of St Thomas the
Apostle, 21 December (now moved to 3 July). I was made deacon
on that day in 1979, as a few of us were in the Church of Ireland. It
was a wonderful and significant day to be launched upon an unsus-
pecting parish: four days before Christmas and yet with the bishop's
charge still ringing in my head, the darkness of winter and the doubt

of Thomas as accompanying themes of preparation. More than four decades later it seems like another world.

But is that what we think of as transformation? Is it a growing out of something from which we have moved on? Surely that is not all there is? No, but I mention it because there is something in the change of external conditions that has an effect upon our internal development. This indeed may well be part of our Advent preparation: the recognition that we are not repeating the same thing year after year as we get ready for Christmas. We are changing. We consider the transforming of society, the call to embrace the values of the kingdom of God, the vision which Jesus came to proclaim, often from the Scriptures of his day, and which was fulfilled by his very presence.

You and I are not mere bystanders in this projection of renewal on a tired and sinful world. The 2020s follow a decade during which the world finally woke up to climate change, absorbed a worldwide pandemic with uneven global consequences, saw the United States of America experience a presidency like none other and the UK, after years of bitter argument, leave the European Union and lose a much-loved monarch. We wait, as surely we must, in awe at what is about to happen, as we reflect upon the vision of the prophets of long ago in a reformed world more than two thousand years after Christ's birth. We know that the key is the Incarnation. The reality of God becoming human in the person of Jesus may be incomprehensible even in a single lifetime, but we have some days left in Advent to do what we can, that is to try to understand what this miracle implies. So we pray for sight to glimpse the glory that is being revealed and for the ability to listen to messages as they are delivered to the ears of those who wait.

I am with Isaiah as one who longs to hear and to be able to see what is not beyond me. Today I confess my lack of attention coupled with a desire for more than I can bear: 'Lord, allow me this I pray: the patience and humility to follow the path of all your servants that leads us to Bethlehem. Reveal what you will to me, and make me learn from it.'

Day 7

Saturday

'O people in Zion, inhabitants of Jerusalem,
you shall weep no more.'
Today's reading: Isaiah 30: 19–21, 23–26

If we analysed what we did day by day, breaking down our usage of time, from driving a car to washing, cooking, completing a set number of steps, checking our screen-time, social media contacts etc., we would probably become very introspective and maybe over-anxious as well. Many things we take as a matter of course but some are the result of long-since forgotten thoughts or practices in our past.

When it comes to devotion to Christ, we may rest in equal measure on the practice of our past and the day-to-day life of our particular parish church. So it is that in a penitential season, such as Advent, the stirring of our life of prayer to consider a specific path of preparation brings with it both a reflection on what we are doing and an objective pondering on that for which we are preparing: Easter during Lent, Christmas during Advent.

Reading the prophecies of Isaiah this week, I am conscious that had this been a different kind of book, I would want to look more deeply at the context in which the prophecies appeared, and, specifically, at the person of Isaiah and the way in which his words and his life have been considered over the centuries. In chapter 30, for example, it is clear that the eighth-century prophet is contemplating the fall of

Jerusalem, that may have been a possibility in his day but would become a growing likelihood as the decades passed.

Next week we shall pass on to a different context and a different prophetic voice, but for our purpose they are one and the same as we search the Scriptures for the words that relate, as we see them, to the coming of Christ. This is not the selection that is made to suit individual tastes and beliefs but the carefully analysed stages that have been revealed in the salvation history of the world, focused, as Christians will declare, in the person of Jesus.

Isaiah wrestles with the physical destruction of what the people hold dear as the ultimate purification of a holy people is revealed in adversity, in scattering, in winnowing. The danger of allowing habitual practice to dictate the ways and works of God's people unconsidered for long periods of time is countered by protracted periods of penitence, such as we are in at the moment. But how to make this effective and not an exercise in change for the sake of change at best or self-condemnation at worst is the secret that we shall try and disclose during the course of next week.

SECOND WEEK OF ADVENT

Day 8

'... the word of God came to John the son of Zechariah
in the wilderness ...'
Today's reading: Luke 3:1–6

On pilgrimage to the Holy Land most people descend on one day to the region of the Dead Sea. Here, at the lowest point on earth, lies a stretch of water with no outlet. The water from the Jordan and other much smaller watercourses flows in, and it can only leave by evaporation, which now occurs more quickly than the salt sea is being refreshed due to extraction of fresh water from the Jordan during the course of its way from the Galilee. Near the Dead Sea we have the region of En Gedi, where David spared the life of Saul; the city of Jericho, where Jesus healed Bartimaeus of blindness and Zacchaeus of greed; Masada, the great mountain fortress of Herod; and what is now an important archeological site, Qumran, where the Dead Sea Scrolls were discovered.

The community that existed at Qumran, the Essenes, lived a strictly ascetic life that involved ritual washing several times a day, manual labour and work in the Scriptorium, painstakingly copying manuscripts. It was a community that sought purification, spiritual enlightenment and ultimately the redemption of Israel. It seems likely that John was part of this desert community, at least for a time. The distance from Qumran to the River Jordan is only a few miles, and it was to that part of the Jordan that Jesus would come for baptism.

On the other hand it is a long way from Nazareth: a drive of several hours on today's roads.

It is thought likely that John heard the prompting of God to leave the community and witness publicly to the need for repentance and forgiveness. Luke speaks of him going about the region, so in all likelihood he was in Jericho, built, originally, because of the oasis just to the west of where the Jordan flows into the Dead Sea. This is a significant geographical point for the people of Israel. Overlooked by Mount Nebo, where Moses viewed the Promised Land, and at the point at which Joshua crossed the Jordan with the whole host of Israel. It is here that John called the people to repent and be baptised.

John is an attractive figure but a challenging one as well, for the fearless way in which he proclaimed what he felt called by God to declare to all who came to him. We know too that he was preparing the way for Jesus. The verses from Luke today do not actually announce that fact, but his actions and quotation from Isaiah are indicative of his intention to create a pathway, albeit metaphorically, in the hearts and minds of the crowd for the word spoken by the Lord to find its goal within each individual searching for the way of righteousness.

In Advent we have to think on different planes at the same time but all connected. We prepare to celebrate the birth of Jesus; we are readying ourselves to respond to the beginning of the ministry of Jesus thirty years later, and we have more than an eye to the fulfilment of all things when Jesus returns in glory. John's role may be specific to the second aspect, but his birth, occurring only just before our Lord's, is for another day of reflection later.

Today we take the track to the River Jordan and hear the commanding words of one who, inspired by the Spirit of God, is still a voice with the power to bring the nations to their knees in sorrow for their sins and to remind individuals that forgiveness follows repentance and a straight and level path aids the way to the living God.

Day 9

Monday

'Say to those who are of a fearful heart,
"Be strong, do not fear!"'
Today's reading: Isaiah 35

A selection of the verses of Isaiah 35 (like a number of other Scriptural texts) have been arranged as one of the canticles for use in daily devotional acts of worship under the title *A Song of the Wilderness*, taken from the opening verse, 'The wilderness and the dry land shall be glad; the desert shall rejoice and blossom'. The words of the verses that follow continue the flow like the poetry it is; its meaning searching the crevices of every situation, crying out for renewal, everywhere where love and life can penetrate the impervious skin of those hardened by cynicism, sin, lack of hope or the imprisonment of the spirit for whatever reason. Isaiah, in one of his great prophecies of a joyful future, sweeps us along with the positive and refreshing message that all will be well.

This is a great chapter before us today. It makes us count our blessings as we continue into this second week of Advent, but it also opens our eyes to what is happening to others as the season of the Church's year slips from the newness of a fresh start eight days ago to the culmination of all things in Christ Jesus. The reality of course is that many of us have the power to make things happen for others by just a little effort or a comparatively small amount of money. We can become hardened by appeals and upset by cold-callers to our door, or, more likely these days, through the many ways we can be reached through a variety of media. Some people have been put off by the aggressive fund-raisers employed by some charities. However, we are in control of our own resources and can help create the vision of Isaiah in lands that have millions of people living without hope.

The prophet is not predicting a spiritual renewal for the people of Israel, he is indicating the hope there is for the outward manifestation of God's blessing upon a land or upon individuals that are blighted. As children of the kingdom of God – daily we pray for its coming – we have a joyful desire to see all humanity receive the blessings that Isaiah holds so beautifully before us in the words of chapter 35. The examples Isaiah gives are these things: water in the desert, sight for the blind, the blossoming of the barren lands, weak hands and feeble knees made strong. Taking renewed hope from Isaiah's images we find fresh courage and resources and place them where our desire and prayers lie. Without our response they will be just sentiment and an unlikely hope, for how else may they be fulfilled?

In the coming days we shall read more of Isaiah's vision for a land that is at peace and blessed with prosperity, but today we turn our hearts and minds to the fearful of this world and how we can support them during these days of preparation and penitence. If we are true to ourselves during the course of Advent then we should look not just to ourselves, and how we as individuals stand before Christ as the Festival of Christmas approaches, but how we are united in love with the fallen of the world: one with them in their pain, one with them in the forsaken Son of God, crucified before the eyes of the world for all humanity.

Day 10

Tuesday

'A voice says, "Cry out!" And I said, "What shall I cry?"'
Today's reading: Isaiah 40:1–11

In 2017 my wife and I took the decision to move from Belfast to Swanage in Dorset and for me to relinquish the role of Dean of Belfast and become a team rector in Salisbury diocese. The urge to stay in Belfast was strong, but there were good reasons to move across the water as well, and we sought over some months to resolve what we thought was the right thing to do. Subsequently, we were able to see that the move was, as hoped, guided and providential, though not easy.

A dramatic change of place can challenge our adaptability, to what degree are we able to part with things we love and embrace the unfamiliar? Many of these changes are obvious, but the more subtle changes brought about by the sounds and sights and smells of a new place affect us subconsciously. During the early weeks of the pandemic restrictions, in the spring of 2020, people became more aware of their natural environment. Today, let us consider the sounds, scents and sights that affect us whether coming or going, or just standing still.

The cause of much of the sound that comes to our ears, as we walk the streets of a town or city, is the result of modern technology. Imagine for a moment sitting in a coffee shop or travelling by whatever means from place to place. We are so used to the sounds of everything from traffic to piped music, the chatter of others and the constant interjection of anything from the wind blowing in the trees to an aircraft flying overhead or a passing flock of birds. There is a staggering amount of noise that we are attuned to automatically, but it is good sometimes to unthread the sounds and sights around us, to use our senses consciously.

This is as easy to do in an urban street as it is in the countryside. It may be that we become more aware of the bleep of the pedestrian crossing or the gathering starlings on a December day at dusk, catch the light of a bicycle lamp or overhear someone's music playing too loudly through their earphones. By the seashore it could be the breaking of the waves, the cry of an oystercatcher or herring gull, often the wind buffeting our clothes or the rub of our waterproofs against each other. We are some way or other brought more in touch with the world around us. Our ears and eyes are becoming trained to notice more than we might otherwise, but our other senses are sure to come along with those that work on sight and sound. We lick salty lips, smell the air and know what we are smelling; touch the earth, the roughness of brick and bark, the slimy wetness of a pebble, the grit of the dust of the ground, whether beach, woodland path or the tarmac that covers acres of our cities.

Isaiah is a poet of the living world but still he sees and feels the inanimate: the roughness of the ground, its unevenness and its gradients. Once he is on the subject of living things his words flow with life; we are like grass, like the flowers of the field, as the fading beauty of all life, that which cries out for renewal from the ruination of human striving in warfare and sin, in pain and fear, in a wilderness of despair; drifting, wandering from the paths of the Good Shepherd. We listen hard to Isaiah's words of comfort, watch for the coming of the guide and then, in our turn, we too cry, announcing the coming of the Saviour, tender words of hope that days of iniquity and wrongdoing may be put behind us. We may rest in the strength of the Lord our God and be led by the shepherd to the place of reconciliation and forgiveness.

Day 11

Wednesday

'but those who wait for the Lord shall renew their strength;
they shall mount up with wings like eagles; they shall run and
not be weary; they shall walk and not faint.'
Today's reading: Isaiah 40: 25–31

Christmas is now in full swing, if this December is like any other. The shops are full of everything except what you want, online things become unavailable between being placed in 'your basket' and getting to the check-out, and out in the real world the school teachers are tense with the final few days before the holidays, whilst children are excited with expectation and parents fraught with getting everything ready and right. Some people inconveniently have a birthday about now too, and others are sorrowful because Christmas brings them the remembrance of past grief. These days are surely more filled with a range of emotions than at any time of the year; frequently all of a mix, which complicates the 'normal' days that make up early-to-mid Advent. That's just it, isn't it? There are no 'normal' days. We may expect Advent to follow a pattern, and we work our way through it, literally religiously, but find that the days evaporate like water on the boil, and we are drying up rather than making the most of an exciting time. We shouldn't worry too much. Thus it ever was.

Rather than worrying that all is not what it 'should' be – whatever that is – let us take Isaiah's advice and wait on the Lord. Isaiah chapter 40 verse 31 is a really encouraging word of Scripture. Yesterday we were listening and crying out, sensitising ourselves to what is affecting our senses already; today we are bidden to lift our eyes and see. We are to consider the creation and the Creator. Like Job at the end of his consideration of life's transience and God's providence, we are inevitably left speechless at the contemplation of life itself. The joy of heaven awaits the servant of God, but in the waiting on the Lord there is a promise of renewed strength for the journey.

The symbol of St John and that presented on many Church lecterns is not just an eagle; it is an eagle taking flight. The wings are outstretched, the talons lifting from the earth, the eye alive with acute sight. In waiting on Christ, whether in the darkness of a sorrow recalled or in the joy of celebration and achievement, or even in the quiet moment of contemplative prayer, the wings of the eagle will carry us to the mountain top where weariness and faintness will pass away.

There is a moment in December when the dates go into double figures, i.e. when we reach the tenth day of the month. This has always seemed like a tipping point for my wife and me. Usually one of us says, 'Well, not long now and so much to do.' The doors on the Advent calendar become easier to find and the jobs are being ticked off. At Church the carol service preparation is reaching its final pitch as lessons are distributed and the choir gets used to singing Advent hymns on a Sunday and practising Christmas Carols through the week. And we are supposed to sit and wait? Yes, that is a task too. Write a list of what has to be done. Leave it to one side for ten minutes and just wait. Breathe deeply and gently and know that Christ inspires the heart that seeks him.

Day 12

Thursday

'For I, the Lord your God, hold your right hand'
Today's reading: Isaiah 41:13–20

This is an interesting passage that is before us today. It speaks of the people being in the hand of God, and they, being weak and fearful and as a 'worm' (verse 14), will be put in a position of power. The second half of the reading specifies the poor and needy; within the sovereignty of God they will be as blessed as any other people. The verses that we are contemplating demonstrate the use of power and its effects. During the opening two decades of the twenty-first century there has been a sense that the world order has changed. The staggering events of 11 September 2001 gave way to twenty years of the US and its allies transforming life in Afghanistan. In 2021, all remaining US forces in the country were dramatically withdrawn. The consequences of holding military power over others has been exposed in all its ambiguities in many areas of the world and important legacy issues of imperialism have been brought to light. As we consider these things in Advent, inevitably we do so in relation to the interplay of the strength of the human institution – as reflected in the regime of Herod – and the strength, or otherwise, of God's expression of the divine path in the way of Christ's appearance, presenting the gateway to human salvation, ultimately through the Incarnation.

Isaiah's words reach us with a magisterial sense of the presence of God. The people of God will be lifted up and held in power that they may express to the very crushing of the mountains, whilst the poor of the land will not just be fed and watered, the whole country from the desert to the heights above will be transformed, because he has heard the voice of their distress.

I am going to introduce the first of the Advent antiphons or refrains on the Magnificat today and in relation to this reading. Traditionally the Advent antiphons are used from 17 December until Christmas Eve for each day at evening prayer. Each introduces and then expands upon a title for Christ in a way that explains its purpose. We sing them in hymn form too as, 'O come, O come Emmanuel', and they may be read as part of the liturgy of an Advent carol service or Advent procession in cathedrals and parishes that provide such a service at this time of the year – in early Advent normally.

Though there is slight variation, usually seven of these refrains are used, and I will mention them between now and Christmas in the form and order that is most familiar to me, which is sourced from *Celebrating Common Prayer*, the Franciscan daily services book from the 1990s that has been supplanted by more contemporary publications but remains a fine devotional guide.

The first antiphon, taking a great Old Testament theme of the divine, creative intelligence lying behind all things, runs: **'O Wisdom, coming forth from the mouth of the Most High, and reaching mightily from one end of the earth to the other, ordering all things well: come and teach us the way of prudence.'** This refrain, said before and after a reading or the Magnificat, sets the tone for that passage and links the prophetic voice from the past with our thoughts today on the Son of God who is to be made flesh for us.

There is a strong tradition in the Old Testament and Apocryphal 'Wisdom' books (e.g. Proverbs, Ecclesiastes and Ecclesiasticus, which we shall read from on Saturday) of the Spirit of God acting as a personification of the ultimate wisdom that governs all things. As such the Lord operates as a sharp sword in division and judgement and so orders the affairs of the world. Christ's coming in the meekness and lowliness of the stable at Bethlehem does not negate this power to order and direct and judge. The antiphon bids us seek the way of 'prudence' that is essentially to live within the knowledge and recognition of that Wisdom; Isaiah's words today make that a compelling desire.

Day 13

Friday

'O that you had paid attention to my commandments!'
Today's reading: Isaiah 48:17–19

There is a very effective line in the sixth chapter of the prophecy of
Hosea. The prophet is bemoaning the fact that the people's love for
God is shallow. He speaks the words of God as poignantly and beautifully but as sadly and critically as this: 'Your love for me is like the
morning mist, like the dew that goes early away.' Comparing prophets is like comparing poets, and both Isaiah and Hosea were both of
these things; they can say the same thing in a range of different and
most importantly of all very telling ways. In other words the message
may come steeped in metaphor and simile, but it will hit you between
the eyes nonetheless.

We have been through a period of human history where image has
almost taken over from the pure spoken word, but with the advent of
the short text message, or tweet, or some other sound-bite, the power
of the spoken or written word to confront or change people's minds
has been recaptured. What we say and how we say it may have changed
in idiom and form, but it is something wonderful and can be terrifying. Some people may date by text and split up by email, but lovers are
touched by spoken words and the silence that comes from their
absence. Let us for a moment relate these thoughts to our prayers.
Prayers are shaped in quietness, in the silence of our hearts or written
for public use into petitions and collects; more simply and profoundly

they are offered in raised heart and soul. By so doing, we give and receive, sometimes entirely without the conscious intervention of the mind, which is stilled in our deepest moment of devotion.

Let's take another Advent antiphon and see where this leads us with these verses: **'O Adonai, and leader of the house of Israel, who appeared to Moses in the fire of the burning bush and gave him the law on Sinai: come and redeem us with an outstretched arm.'** The Lord appeared to Moses and each time came the challenge to listen and obey. At the burning bush he tried to wriggle out of what to him was too much to ask; on Sinai he received the commandments; his problem then was to deliver them to a people unready to accept them.

In 2012 I climbed Mount Sinai with eleven other pilgrims. In so many ways it is like any other desert mountain, but as we stood at the top and munched our Kendal Mint Cake and took photographs we were alone. Everyone else had gone up for the sunrise, but we went later because we had arrived very late the night before. So there was time, when the Russian and Eastern European pilgrims (of which there were many) were already admiring the ancient icons at St Catherine's Monastery below us, to consider the latent power of this place to affect our lives.

To hearken to commandments does involve an engagement with the mind and a real decision to obey, but it equally affects the inner journeying of the soul toward God. As Moses stood at the burning bush, his sandals were cast aside for the holy ground upon which he stood. As the tablets of the law were inscribed by God for the people, the recognition of the place of holiness, of godliness, of worship is wrapped up in the moment. Every twist of this day's reflection has it, from the dew of Hosea's metaphor, through the silence of anticipation to the wordless encounter of the mountain-top experience. The power of commandment to inspire commitment as well as obedience is vital to our appreciation of how faith becomes devotion.

33

Day 14

Saturday

'Then Elijah arose, a prophet like fire, and
his word burned like a torch.'
Today's reading: Ecclesiasticus 48:1–4, 9–11

Ecclesiasticus 48:1–4, 9–11

Then Elijah arose, a prophet like fire,
  and his word burned like a torch.
He brought a famine upon them,
  and by his zeal he made them few in number.
By the word of the Lord he shut up the heavens
  and also three times brought down fire.
How glorious you were, Elijah, in your wondrous deeds!
  Who can boast as you can?
[You] who were taken up by a whirlwind of fire
  in a chariot with horses of fire,
who were prepared at the appointed time
  to calm wrath before it breaks out in fury,
to turn the hearts of parents to their children
  and to restore the tribes of Jacob.
Happy are those who saw you
  and were adorned in love!
    For we also shall surely live.

The verses from the apocryphal book of Ecclesiasticus or 'The Wisdom of Jesus Son of Sirach', appointed to be read today, may not be easily available to everyone, so they are printed in full above. Elijah and fire are easily connected, but these words will not be familiar to many of us. The reason for their inclusion is entirely in relation to John the Baptist who we will encounter again tomorrow.

We recall, through more well-known texts, from the First and Second Books of Kings, that both Elijah and his protégé Elisha were *feared* (as in the fear of God is the beginning of wisdom) for being able to call down fire from heaven – a very disconcerting gift in the eyes of the fainthearted. But then again, as with Moses, Elijah's mountaintop companion at Christ's transfiguration, this prophet himself was strictly for the committed. There is no doubt that John the Baptist was a similar type of person to Elijah, but, getting away from the fire motif, the comparison is more due to the robust way in which these men were prepared to get their message across. The word coming from Elijah's mouth and 'burning like a torch' could easily be matched with what we shall hear from John the Baptist in some verses from Luke tomorrow.

In the meantime we rest with Elijah and ask ourselves how he prepares us, from his place in Israel's salvation history, for the coming of the Messiah. The answer, to my mind, lies in the refining and renewing of the people through testing. The prophet sought not only during the years of drought and famine but more particularly in his contest with the prophets of Baal on Mount Carmel to express the purity of the worship of God, which would not hold the dross of insincerity or inconsistency.

His words, burning like a torch, are indicative by their very nature of a prophet inclined to see his role as pivotal. The evidence from the latter chapters of the First Book of Kings suggest that he did indeed see himself as possessing a central position in bringing the people back to Yahweh. His sense of anti-climax after the Carmel challenge, which caused him to flee from Ahab and Jezebel, something he would not have done earlier, suggests that knew his time to pass on the flame (to continue the burning image of the message) was subconsciously already there to be confirmed on Mount Sinai.

There is something very comforting in this transitional but ever forward-looking role for the prophet as the present is held up in relation to the past, but with the eyes set firmly on what is to come. The days of Advent are coming and going, and we may think that to spend a few moments with the prophets of old is little use as the demands of Christmas approaching are all around us. Have you done this and have you done that? Well, probably not. In fact I had better get going, but before I do, I will pause and spare a moment for one whose words burned like a torch and to know that I too can hold the words of promise through the distracting hours of busyness as I recall the towering figure of Elijah and listen tomorrow to the words of St John the Baptist, which I know will be burning too.

THIRD WEEK OF ADVENT

Day 15

The Third Sunday of Advent

'As the people were filled with expectation and all were
questioning in their hearts concerning John, whether he might
be the Messiah, John answered all of them by saying, 'I baptise
you with water, but one who is more powerful than I is
coming; I am not worthy to untie the strap of his sandals.
He will baptise you with the Holy Spirit and fire.'
Today's reading: Luke 3:7–18

Yesterday, we recalled the tradition that likens John the Baptist to the
prophet Elijah. In fact we more than recalled it; we began to draw
out the parallel. They are both portrayed as similarly dressed, standing alone for God in the midst of great wickedness. Elijah's words
were 'burning like a torch'. Now we witness John the Baptist speaking of fire in relation to Jesus, not himself; I dare say that there are
those who would claim that his words were as burning and torch-
like as anyone's and that is the reason for all that questioning in
people's hearts.

On this fifteenth day of Advent, as we approach Christmas, and
taking the words and person of John the Baptist to our hearts, we
listen to his words and try to understand his place in this scene of
proclamation, repentance, forgiveness and redemption. John does not
mince his words, but he finds a receptive audience. These are people
who are ready for a new start, tired of their old ways and seeking to
be renewed.

As we anticipate at this time not the coming of Jesus as an adult but as a baby in a stable in Bethlehem, how is this helpful? We have much to think about in these days of Advent. Between cataclysmic climate change warnings, economic forecasts, the long-term effects on individuals and nations of a global pandemic, the reality of ongoing conflicts, one could be forgiven for assuming that there is not much good news to be heard in the world on this third Sunday of Advent. But when we listen to John the Baptist in the Gospel of Luke today, we find that his words of good news also involve a large degree of potential pain. He is insisting that the good news is for those who are prepared to make the hard choices in terms of life-style change, and there are fearful penalties for those who do not comply. This is John the Baptist at his determined and utterly convincing best. He did prepare the way for Jesus, not just in providing the baptism of repentance but by breaking up the soil of peoples' consciences; our Lord himself took many a farming image to press home his points of teaching later, including the parable of the sower, but here John is looking at fruits, not the fresh green shoots of new growth but the fruitless tree and the chaff, comparing them with the fruiting tree and the wheat being gathered into the granary.

John is one of the most grounded of New Testament characters. He has a good understanding of his role and whilst not recognising the detail of the Messiah's teaching and ministry, he saw very clearly what its main object was to be. Considering that he may well have been living in a desert community for some years, he shows a remarkable grasp of what was needed of him and of the desires, weaknesses and longings of those who came to listen to him and to be baptised. Returning to the theme of good news coming with pain, we see that those who were going wrong for some reason or other in their lives were being encouraged to accept the good news and its consequences immediately and with conviction. What everyone who listens to John the Baptist receives is hope. There is always hope, but hope that is realised is like a re-birth, a new life, a fresh injection of energy.

There is good news: the kingdom of God is at hand. The Messiah is soon to appear. For all who find salvation in Jesus there is hope, joy, anticipation and thanksgiving. There is also a challenge to our lives and desires, a motivation to make changes where necessary and not simply to put off the inevitable to another day.

Day 16

Monday

'The oracle of Balaam son of Beor, the oracle of the man whose eye is clear, the oracle of one who hears the words of God ...'
Today's reading: Numbers 24:2–7, 15–17

The Book of Numbers does not appear often in the lectionary. It is a book of wonderings and wanderings, which charts the people of Israel on their journey from the land of Egypt, escaping from the hand of Pharaoh, through the Red Sea and the desert of Sinai to reach the Promised Land. It took forty years for this to happen, and Numbers tells us why.

The wilderness experience subsequent to the Exodus carried the people around the Sinai peninsula and up through the modern Kingdom of Jordan. The Book of Numbers has been divided into three parts: from the beginning of chapter 1 until chapter 10 verse 10 we read of the Hebrew people encamped at Sinai and preparing to leave on the journey to the oasis of Kadesh. They then gathered their forces and decided that the time had come to enter the Promised Land, consequently they made an abortive attack on Canaan from the south, through the Negev.

If you consider the geography of the region, this would make a lot of sense as, short of hugging the coast, it is the most straightforward route from Egypt to Israel, inland from the Gaza strip, straight into the heart of the country. It didn't work; they could not take the country that way. The story of this failed attack, that we hardly ever consider, forms chapter 10 verse 11 to chapter 21 verse 13. The remainder of the book charts the progress of the Israelites in travelling from Kadesh through Transjordan to approach Canaan from the east.

Eventually they decided to go the long way around and attack Canaan from what I suppose was perceived as its weaker eastern flank. There was a great highway that ran up through the eastern side of the river Jordan and the Dead Sea. This was an important trade route, called the King's Highway, and there were a few important but small kingdoms to be encountered and crossed on the way, primarily Edom and Moab. We were told that they decided to go round the land of Edom, presumably to avoid battle and get onto the main trade route from much further south by the Red Sea. This is a bit like going from Belfast to Sligo via Cork, or Swanage to London via St David's, and remember, they were doing it on foot. And the writer of Numbers tells us 'the people became impatient on the way, and spoke against God and against Moses'. Is it any wonder?

They could not avoid battle and the opposing nations had their prophets too. Balaam being one of them. He is called upon by his king to curse the people of Israel, but he finds that he can do nothing but bless them and some of his words form the reading today. As we consider how God can use those who oppose his people to ultimately bring a blessing, we do so with great care, knowing how the passage to that ultimate blessing may be hard and painful. St Paul presided over the persecution of the Church before his conversion; Herod led the wise men to Bethlehem, but also murdered the babies there; Judas, Caiaphas and Pilate all played their part in the crucifixion of Jesus, but did they do so in accordance with the will of God? Indirectly yes, but surely Judas was no more born to betray Jesus, than was John the Baptist to lose his head ...

Day 17

Tuesday

'For I will leave in the midst of you a people humble and lowly.'
Today's reading: Zephaniah 3: 1,2, 9–13

Let us look at another of the Advent refrains: **'O root of Jesse, standing as a sign to the people, before whom kings shall shut their
mouths and the nations shall seek: come and deliver us and do
not delay.'**

The words of deliverance and restoration are never far from the
Advent hope, which may also bring the terrifying prospect of calam-
ity and destruction. The notion of a world spiralling to its end and in
the thrall of Satan has been a consciously accepted understanding
from the words of many of the prophets and Zephaniah is no excep-
tion. He begins his prophecy with these uncompromising words, 'I
will utterly sweep away everything from the face of the earth, says
the Lord.' 'I will sweep away humans and animals; I will sweep away
the birds of the air and the fish of the sea.' There is more of the same.

   Now if you are about to go to your work's Christmas night out, are
pottering about looking for the Christmas decorations, or are about
to go shopping, it may be that connecting with the end of the world
is a bit difficult. But that is the thing about Advent isn't it? We are
never ready, never ready to take the great themes of this season to
heart, for the sheer busyness of these days. So easily Advent slips into
Christmas again and the season is lost once more. Maybe to have a

penitential season *after* Christmas rather than before it would be the answer, but I am not convinced that there is a better way.

In a way it goes back to the reason for writing this book. There are far fewer Advent books than those written for Lent. Partially that may be because it has a varied number of days and there are some tricky themes to interweave, but primarily because there is a general eroding of Advent because of the difficulty in maintaining any kind of penitential discipline, unless we happen to live alone and are socially a recluse. The answer for most of us seems to lie in accepting the inevitable compromise that communities in Britain and Ireland have created in building towards the climax of Christmas Day – and then it's over – instead of embracing a season of Christmas after days of restrained preparation, holding back until the mysterious wonder of Christmas Eve arrives. Much of the Church in these islands, has embraced this concept through school and community activities in bringing Christmas so deliberately into Advent, allowing the days of Christmas itself to be celebrated as family times. Yet at the same time, slightly uneasy with this eroding of importance of Advent tries to create a parallel corridor of personal devotion, supported with strongly themed Advent liturgies (such as Salisbury Cathedral's "Service of Light" that is so popular that it has to be run twice, and is full to the doors each night, and similar Advent processions and carol services are now common). The hope is that the desire to experience this kind of liturgy for Advent will lead individuals to explore the reasons for the appearance of Christ more thoroughly, and to devote some time each day to the contemplation of the stepping stones that are placed for the Advent journey through the rushing stream of Christmas celebration. It is possible to do both. Each day of this book is a stepping stone toward a reflective and prayerful celebration of the Christmas season. We could see the link in terms of strengthening relationships, both human and divine; prayerfully approaching the mystery of the Incarnation, whilst taking five minutes at some time each day with a relative or friend, as an opportunity to sustain and, in some sense enhance, personal relationships around the festivities.

Today we have the prophecy of Zephaniah and our hope to see in the midst of us a people who are humble and lowly, a people who could have recognised in the shepherd son of Jesse a man born to be king; it is a hope that silences in awe the turmoil of the nations and prepares the way for the King of kings and Lord of lords, Jesus, the Son of the Most High.

As the world comes to terms with the challenges of the times in which we live, so the vision of the Old Testament prophets is re-examined in the light of the Christian understanding of how things are seen providentially. This not only opens the hearts of God's people to the ways of the kingdom but opens minds to see that whilst the crises of our day are arguably of an unprecedented scale, humanity's ability to discern and look through Christ's eyes at opportunities and possibilities is as great as ever. At this point in Advent the reality of the Incarnation is central to these thoughts, and whilst today a stump or a root is the description we are given of hope and promise, it is a picture of resilience and more – a new beginning.

Day 18

Wednesday

'I form light and create darkness, I make weal and create woe;
I the Lord do all these things.'
Today's reading: Isaiah 45:6b–8, 18, 21b–end

The themes of light and darkness are especially present as we approach Christmas, though at no time in the Christian year are they absent from our understanding of the presence of God and that of evil. At Easter the bringing of the light into the darkness of the Church on Easter Eve and the burning of the new Paschal Candle are powerful indications of the new life in Christ, as the Resurrection is proclaimed. During Advent we look to the coming of the Light of the World. The image of a state of darkness produced in God's good creation by humans, requiring the Light of Christ to dispel, is also an extremely clear picture of what is happening.

St John, in the prologue to his account of the gospel, virtually inter-changes light and life, whilst drawing both a comparison with and distinction between John the Baptist and Jesus. This certainly leaves us with the impression that the light of Christ is unique and not just a matter of an illumination that may be temporary. There is also a parallel with the period between Good Friday and Easter Day in our Advent preparation, when we are asked to consider the prisoner. That sense of confinement and the promise of release is proclaimed in another Advent antiphon: '**O Key of David, and sceptre of the**

house of Israel, who opens and no one can shut, who shuts and no one can open: Come and bring the prisoners from the prison house, those who dwell in darkness and the shadow of death.'

To consider Advent as a time to promote release and to rejoice in it happening is an opportunity not to be missed amidst all the holly and paper-chains. This is a good moment to concentrate on the causes that bring about release to those held in captivity for whatever reason and under whatever circumstances. It falls happily into this season and perfectly with our Isaiah reading for today. There are many in the world who know captivity of one kind or another and have little if any hope in their hearts and minds that they might be released. For some it comes because of their courage in challenging the confining and oppressive nature of the regimes under which they and their families are forced to live. Others do not even have this narrow choice between capitulation or danger, so vulnerable and weak is their position. Confronted with the human rights abuses of our day, the Christian has the opportunity to support the lobbying bodies that keep the flame of hope alive for the oppressed peoples of the world.

Meanwhile, during these advancing Advent days, the hopes of the Christian world are gathering about a small town called Bethlehem. Today it is hemmed in by a security wall; the presence of the wall may be justified by security considerations, but as it is built against Palestinian homes rather than halfway between them and Israeli settlements, it is particularly oppressive and threatening. Yet in this place the Prince of Peace was born and preparations will be advanced to celebrate once again the coming of the Saviour, who announced the opening of the eyes of the blind and the release of the captive.

'Shower, O heavens, from above, and let the skies rain down righteousness; let the earth open, that salvation may spring up, and let it cause righteousness to sprout up also; I the Lord have created it.' Verse 8 brings us the picture of the coming of the gift of righteousness: raining down from the heavens, springing up from the earth. It brings an undeniably renewed quality of life and is part of the vision of the coming of the kingdom of God.

Day 19

Thursday

'For the mountains may depart and the hills be removed, but my steadfast love shall not depart from you, and my covenant of peace shall not be removed, says the Lord, who has compassion on you.'
Today's reading: Isaiah 54:1–10

We can hardly approach Christmas without spending a day considering our responsibility to love our neighbour, because God's love for us is about to be outpoured in the Incarnation of Christ. Isaiah may have a vision of God's love and compassion and peace as being eternal and ever present with his people, but we have love incarnate as our constant companion on the way.

This is not just in response to an example, even though that example may be the perfect expression of divine love as the precursor of all human love. A few days ago we touched on the first Advent antiphon that speaks of Wisdom coming forth from the mouth of the most high. But what does it mean to have wisdom? How is wisdom acquired? In the attitude of faith, wisdom is gained through love. Chiara Lubich, founder of the Focolare Movement, once likened this to the process of generating electricity on a bicycle using a dynamo: 'As a bicycle light comes on when you pedal, so wisdom lights upon us when we love.'

Now Isaiah is witnessing to the love of God being present with his people. This helps to remind us that the light and life that we receive through the outpouring of the love of God is manifested before we even begin to take the first faltering steps towards the demonstration of love in our lives. That manifestation is expressed in Christ's presence in our lives and the Holy Spirit inspiring us, and love is generated if we will allow the pure selfless person of Jesus to weave his will into ours.

Thomas Merton, in *New Seeds of Contemplation*, put it this way, 'We must learn to realise that the love of God seeks us in every situation, and seeks our good. His inscrutable love seeks our awakening.'

'Seeks our awakening' brings the source of love to the harmonious but unsettling reaction that makes 'desire' such an alluring but potentially destructive quality to devotional practice and Christian life. So, let us consider how this works as daily we pray and speak and act. Desire draws us into meditation on the love of God. This emotional focus illuminates the Scriptures, for we are seeking, hoping, being swept up with the need to express our innermost longing. This is where the potential danger lies, for there are darker desires that compete with the desire for the mystical union with Christ. We find our equilibrium in the same way as a child learning to swim or someone walking along a precipitous path, the 'Don't think about your head going under' or 'Don't look down' are countered by the instructor or leader repeating over and over, 'Just keep your eyes on me!'

That word of direction is also a word of comfort and encouragement. It allows the desire for Christ to become the key in drawing us into a love that is wisdom personified and incarnated in Jesus and realised within us in the Eucharist. **'O Dayspring, splendour of light eternal and sun of righteousness: Come and enlighten those who dwell in darkness and the shadow of death.'** Yes, the meaning of this fifth Advent antiphon is revealed in the silence of those who live a life of love even in the terrors of night.

Day 20

Friday

'For my thoughts are not your thoughts, nor are your ways my ways, says the Lord.'
Today's reading: Isaiah 55:1–3a; 6–8

My six years as Dean of Belfast taught me many things but some that have been as unexpected as they were important. Among these I would put the effect of wrestling with the intractable question of what to do when you have to publicly commemorate or celebrate some event or individual life that is, to put it mildly, highly controversial. People are watching, ready to criticize you; they are expecting the commemoration or celebration to be done in a particular way, suiting their theological position, understanding of history, or view of the event or person in question. Knowing this makes you very careful, careful to do things and express things as you believe they should be done and said, rather than the way that will produce the most effective response from those applying the most pressure.

The premise that no one gets everything right is a good starting point, followed by the reminder that no one is naturally thinking God's thoughts or acting in the way that would be his way. This has a deeply humbling aspect to it as well, as we try to avoid the gung-ho, 'Well this is how it is going to be' or alternatively the over-compliant way of simply fulfilling expectations.

We have touched already on how most churches have accepted the need to absorb the inevitable social and commercial aspects of Christmas into the days of Advent. Within the mystery of contemplating the miracle of what is actually being celebrated at Christmas comes the need to connect with and share the joy of those whose Christmas has no religious content and those who may be deeply religious but of another faith, who are generously sharing with their Christian friends.

In these situations of sharing, we can make serious steps in understanding where mutual respect allows us to compare our outlook and beliefs. Dialogue is best begun by dwelling on the aspects of Mary and Joseph that reflect their response to the visits of the archangel Gabriel, whilst, at the same time, drawing the wider vision of the whole of creation being included in the gathering act of God. We are reminded of the cosmic view of the wise men beginning their journey, which is in the form of a pilgrimage, and John the Baptist, whose role is moral and spiritual but no less central. That is a lot of different thoughts to thread together on our way to Bethlehem.

Crucially we acknowledge that we are all learning and not claiming a knowledge that we do not have. Can we honestly say that we would have done it this way: having the Saviour of the World born into obscurity and in the midst of the animals of a stable? Every part of this story, from the magnetic pull of Bethlehem to the humility and danger of the Nativity story as it unfolds, speaks of a plan devised by God whose ways are not our ways. For us Christmas may be a sentimental time. If, however, we take seriously and pay close attention to the preceding ages of prophecy, there is little doubt that the incredible account of the birth of Jesus reflects a vulnerability – a significant risk. The child is trusted to a young mother and a human father that have been chosen for their particular qualities of faith and trust, but at every stage they needed to receive and follow the guidance given to them by angelic words.

That, ultimately, is how the ways and words of God become those of the Christian, when faith and trust engage with what is being asked of us, as we turn in prayer to the Father and seek to follow the ways of his Son. The path is not always easy and frequently may take us into places, both literally and metaphorically, where we would rather not go, but it is in the doing and the talking through that the way is found, in the company of others.

Day 21

Saturday

'... the obedience of the nations shall be his.'
Today's reading: Genesis 49:2, 8–10

When I was very little I went to school in Blackheath, where I was born, to what was then a relatively new institution, set up in an old house by two ladies of an evangelical Christian background, for the education of young children. It was called the 'Pointer School' in my day and has now morphed into 'Pointers' with a very smart uniform, rather expensive fees and an attractive website. I recall little of it but one or two formative moments do flash past from time to time. One of my first reports declares, in careful copperplate handwriting, 'John has settled down into an habitual "old stager" ... In the main he is rather quiet, but there is a riotous side to him which is well worth watching. He knows his own mind.' So it goes on; though I do smile at the, 'jumping presents an obvious obstacle'. I was just beyond my third birthday and that term was not my first. I am not sure that I showed any aptitude for priesthood then, but, then again ... let's not go there ...

In all the mixed up comings and goings of the Book of Genesis, it ends up with the death of Jacob and the death of Joseph. These two men, father and son, brought the leadership of God's people through some mighty upheavals and not a little controversy. In chapter 49 Jacob is relating to his sons what their future is to be. He makes a lot from a little and concludes with blessing them all before he died. The passage that is appointed for today involves Joseph's brother Judah. His tribe was to be that which would hold the sceptre, the ruling line that would ultimately pass to him who will gain 'the obedience of the nations'. Christians see the saying fulfilled in Jesus, but this is reaching back a long way; it is from so far back in history, that it is like looking back at a glimmer of our young life from old age. It is like another country, and one that has gone through a turmoil of change and development. Yet there is something in a person that never changes; something to which we must adapt, and something that affects the forming of relationships between one another and God.

'O King of the nations, and their desire, the corner-stone making both one: Come and save us, whom you formed from the dust.' As we read this sixth and penultimate antiphon, we take its features and reflect too. The King of the nations naturally draws the obedience of the peoples; their desire is for him; he becomes the corner stone laid upon a foundation already built by God; he comes to save we who are formed from the dust. What lies in the past continues to have a bearing on the present and the future, and Christians map the way to Bethlehem in the words of the prophets of Israel.

FOURTH WEEK OF ADVENT

Day 22

The Fourth Sunday of Advent

'Blessed are you among women and blessed is the
child you will bear!'
Today's reading: Luke 1:39–55

The contemplation of the place of Mary in the salvation history of God's people is not something that can be spelled out in 500 words or so as a day's reflection in this or any other book. Mary the mother of Jesus holds a special place in the life and witness of the Christian Church, and for many her devotion is the inspiration to their life of faith. Consider Mary's calling, and the particular way she received it: in humility, without question, placing herself in a condition of life-long acceptance under authority. This made all the more poignant by her desire to embrace all the consequences of her role, including the anguish and sorrow of which she was warned. How many women, and men too, have willingly sought the path of humble service as they have meditated on the love of God as reflected in Christ but borne out so devotedly by Mary?

In Anglican churches Mary is often most obviously portrayed on traditional Mothers' Union banners: a young woman, holding a child, dressed in blue and white, lilies reflecting purity flank her on either side. Some of these banners are of priceless beauty, lovingly created and standing in the corner of the sanctuary or nave as a symbol of the inspiration of the virgin mother. So, the complexity and importance of Mary's role in the Church grows as we see her next in stained glass windows of the crucifixion: John to one side, Christ crucified in the centre, and Mary, her eyes cast upward in love, her hands clasped in deep distress, stands opposite the beloved disciple to the other side. The issue of how her ethnicity is portrayed – as with Jesus himself – is a relatively recent concern, but one highlighting the level of acceptance of the Westernising of the Biblical scenes, either transposing them into something familiar or creating an imagined vision of how things may have been.

However we overcome the constructions, both visual and descriptive, of previous generations of Christians with a Western outlook, we may find it difficult to understand just how important Mary is to the devotional life of others within and beyond the Christian traditions that have developed over the centuries. This young girl holds the Christian Church in thrall; she captivates us, draws us to her life, not just because she was chosen to bear the Son of God, though that might be considered enough in itself, but because she encapsulates all that we would want to be and yet haven't the courage, strength or even the devotional will to approach. As a result, many appeal to Mary as she does to them, whilst others stand to one side and admire. Her life can hold all of this because she is a pattern, as Christ is the revelation, of the divine-human possibility that carries our faith, transforms our life and creates within us the chance of salvation. All is realised through the cross, but to see what that looks like in daily living, we need look no further than Mary.

Day 23

Monday

'And now you will be silent and not able to speak
until the day this happens ...'
Today's reading: Luke 1:5–25

Incredulity is not a capital offence, but in the eyes of the prophets
of God it had always demonstrated weakness, and Zechariah is in
the company of an archangel, not just a prophet. 'I am Gabriel', he
says, 'I stand in the presence of God, and I have been sent to speak
to you and bring you this good news.' Handling doubt is none too
easy, as Thomas found a few years later, but what we see here is a
struggle with honesty. What is said reflects the state of mind of the
hearer and whether that be Abraham or Elijah, Jonah or Moses,
Jacob, Hannah, Naomi or Ruth, if what we hear has the ring of
truth we can entertain the possibility of the most amazing things,
but it is the recognition of truth that translates incredulity into
possibility.

Numerous parishes and churches, not to mention individuals, have
discovered their answer to prayer coming unexpectedly but, in their
understanding, miraculously, as some undertaking or concern is settled with the unheralded arrival of resources or good news which
transform the situation into something providential. Zechariah
needed just such reassurance at this moment, but he did not receive
it, rather he is struck dumb.

We are few days from Christmas, still holding Advent as a season of preparation, whilst around us the festivities are in full swing. How can these verses from Luke, that tie us into the life of an aged priest and his encounter with Gabriel, bring the last days of penitence before the Christ-mass to life? There is a focus here that may give us just what we need today. For Zechariah it was an imposed silence, but perhaps it was a silence that he needed, to come to terms with Gabriel – not just his words, but even more so, his very presence. 'I stand in the presence of God' is a mighty calling card.

In September 2014 the Archbishop of Canterbury Justin Welby was engaged in a live debate in Bristol Cathedral and was asked by a BBC interviewer whether he ever doubted the existence of God. Very honestly, the Archbishop not only spoke of his doubts, which similarly assail us all at times, but enlarged this to speak of the difficulty Christians have in understanding suffering in the world. The headlines, on websites and news broadcasts, were simple and along these lines: 'Archbishop of Canterbury doubts the existence of God.' Anyone who has spoken to the media will know just how the reporting of what is said can be used selectively. In fact in a pre-recorded interview it must be, because much more is taken than is required, but frequently the selection highlights either the things you don't expect or takes precisely what is said, but it is placed out of its natural context.

Zechariah had to face both things, having emerged from his encounter with Gabriel. What had happened was unexpected, and what he was told was beyond his comprehension, and quite out of the situation and experience with which he was at that moment engaged. He was struck dumb indeed, maybe as a punishment, more likely as an outcome of his mind being stretched beyond the possible. He had time to take it all in, and we have a chance today to think about those hours of pondering, as we in our own time ask the questions: 'What does this all mean?' and 'How can I prepare for something I struggle to understand?' Fortunately, unlike prominent Church leaders, we don't have to answer these questions in front of a camera with a microphone pointing at us. Zechariah's dumbness does prompt us to consider how we can begin to articulate what strikes us with awe but also calls us to reflect and respond.

Day 24

Tuesday

'"I am the Lord's servant", Mary answered.
"May your word to me be fulfilled."'
Today's reading: Luke 1:26–38

This single line attributed to Mary forms the foundation of much of our understanding of what she was truly like. Yesterday we read of Zechariah's incredulity; today, in the following verses Luke's first chapter, we are asked to absorb the announcement of an even more spectacular miracle: a virgin conception, no less than the Son of God, and one who is to be the Saviour. Initially Mary asks quite a similar question to Zechariah. He had used these words to Gabriel: 'How shall I know this for I am an old man, and my wife is advanced in years.' Mary asks: 'How shall this be, since I have no husband.' Zechariah is struck dumb, but Mary receives the answer to her question from the angel.

Our interpretation of this would, I think, be along the lines of: Zechariah's words, though superficially similar to Mary's, have the ring of doubt. 'How shall I know this?' is a request for proof; 'How shall this be?' is a plea of 'Please, explain how this will happen.' It could be also that Gabriel would anticipate a response in faith from this experienced priest and a couple who are recognised as 'righteous before God', whilst in Mary's case the angel is speaking to a young girl, who has little experience in the religious life. However it may be, we know that the words of Mary ring true, and the commitment of her life to the service of the Lord is instant and complete.

This Tuesday, as every day this week, may be Christmas Eve or the day before it, and certainly will be in some years, so each reflection of week four must possess that closeness of anticipation to the Nativity itself. This reading casts us back to 25 March and the Annunciation of the Blessed Virgin Mary. Today's reading is the gospel for that day, whilst the Collect speaks of us having 'known the Incarnation … by the message of an angel', whilst the route to 'the glory of his resurrection' comes through 'his cross and passion', which throws us forward in the Christian year to Holy Week. So a little grounding is needed, or our minds shall flee to somewhere other than where we should be today.

We are grounded by what we may properly describe as the 'Call'; for all that we build into our picture of Mary as a mother whose heart is pierced by a sword of deep sorrow, she is the example to us of the perfect acceptance of the role that she is asked by God to fulfil. We may never lose sight of the youthful mother at Christmas, but neither do we forget the ageless quality of love that allows every one of us to accept a fulfilling calling at any age and at whatever stage of life. Love is the transforming quality that makes us what we are, according to how that love is lived and to whom it is outpoured. In Mary we see the perfection of love directed to God, recognised in this annunciation, experienced in the stable, but more potently and transformatively upon the cross.

Day 25

Wednesday

'When Elizabeth heard Mary's greeting, the baby leaped in her
womb, and Elizabeth was filled with the Holy Spirit.'
Today's reading: Luke 1:39–45

As choirboys, my brothers and I looked forward to the annual choir
carol singing. I am speaking of the 1960s, you understand, when
house-to-house carol singing was expected from church choirs and
streets were quieter. The day of the carol singing involved preparation, though perhaps not quite of a Thomas Hardy order – more like
a scene from Richmal Crompton's *Just William* series. It was generally spent with jam jars, string and candles or with balsa wood, batteries, wire and light fittings from the 'junior electricians kit' from
one of the toy makers of half a century ago. A bit of tinsel, some cel-
lophane and a workable lantern could be knocked up, which would
gradually disintegrate in the evening to come. Then it would be the
gathering at the church, and off we would go with merry step to
the first house. Looking back, I am sure that we didn't realise that
the route was carefully chosen to take in a few 'important' parishio-
ners and those ready to feed the twenty odd choristers with sausage
rolls and Tizer! I suspect we were a fairly odd bunch too, but we sung
our hearts out, and this was just the start. There were the carol
services within a few days and the midnight mass to come. Our
parents thought it was great, us coming in shattered, well after midnight on Christmas Eve. Sleep was inevitable.

Visiting is part of Christmas; it was even part of Mary's adventure that led to the manger and the birth of Jesus. Today we think of her visiting Elizabeth. What is highlighted is joy, surprise, wonder, fulfilment and ultimately all of these things wrapped in unity and love. It is expressed in a few ways in the text: the baby stirring in the womb of Elizabeth, implying that John could respond, even before birth, to the presence of the expectant mother of Jesus; then Elizabeth's words of amazement that Mary should come to see her at all.

We hardly realise what we take in, as we in our own way take steps to visit other people's houses: those of friends and family, those of strangers and neighbours, those of fellow church-goers and maybe those of other faiths with whom we have come to share the main celebrations of our respective religions. As we knock on the door, or ring the bell, with maybe a present or greeting card to hand, perhaps we could spare a thought for this meeting of Mary and Elizabeth: the absence of jealousy, the genuine joy of playing some part together in the mystery of God's amazing plan, the chance to share, with a smile and excitement and, yes, a blessing, with someone else whose life at that moment is crossing ours. We may not have much to give, but as we will all recall from the last verse of the Christmas carol, 'In the bleak mid-winter', it is our heart that is the greatest treasure, and that we can give to the Christ-child by sharing what we have with others.

Day 26

Thursday

'From now on all generations will call me blessed, ...'
Today's reading: Luke 1:46–56

Mary is ever, the 'Blessed' Virgin Mary and has a very special place in the life and devotion of Christians, especially within the Roman Catholic Church and within Anglo-Catholicism, as well as being '*Theotokos*' or the bearer of God in the Orthodox tradition. The fact that she saw herself as blessed is obvious, and that she knew that generations to come would acknowledge that too is something we recite at Evening Prayer each day. From the said words of an individually read evening office to the grandest of choral evensongs, sung in magnificent settings, we proclaim Mary's words of joy, amazement and perhaps above all, her contemplation of humility. What she felt, she was led to by the very turning over in her mind of what was her calling: she was to be the mother of God.

I have four brothers and two sisters. We all have biblical names. In fact, to be precise, we all have New Testament names: Timothy, John, Simon, Paul, Mark, Mary and Elizabeth. When we were young, I imagined that my sisters were named after Queen Mary and Queen Elizabeth, two strong characters in the twentieth-century British monarchy, but truly, my parents chose from the Bible. Mary and Elizabeth are two women whom Luke portrays with strength and tenderness combined: each holding an endearing and deeply rooted love for the other, each passionately consumed by their calling and struck to the core by their blessedness. As they saw it: undeserved, miraculous and utterly and shatteringly humbling.

Mary speaks in her song of blessedness of the poor, the hungry and the lowly, setting them in contrast to the rich and those who have everything. At Christmas there is no doubt that most people are generous beyond their normal habits, not only to their family and friends but also to the stranger and especially to the homeless. There is more going on here than easing one's conscience over eating and drinking whilst others go hungry; we conceive of home and the convivial atmosphere of family and friends, and we dwell on what it means to be blessed. Before we have so much as opened a card or present, laid the table for a meal or offered a drink to a friend, we do some heart-opening and some pondering, or, if we don't we should. Christmas brings sad memories for some and pain and grief to others. We are not all like Mary at this moment experiencing the youthful expectation of a joyful birth and the happiness of fulfilment and building a home. Maybe the sword that was to pierce Mary's heart is already within your own.

The Magnificat has words even for the heart-broken and sorrowful at Christmas, for the Lord, as magnified in the eyes of Mary, is the one who is ever picking up those who are cast down and bearing the weight of holiness and blessedness even for those who cannot imagine such things for themselves. His mercy and strength are apparent to Mary, and they are transforming in the bearing, real as we seek them, binding us in safety as in St Patrick's vision of the Trinity as a shield. Let us pray now for the blessedness of Mary to be known in the hearts of all who are hurting today, and through it may angels bear them to hear the shepherds in the fields, the animals in the stable, the first cry of the Christ-child and experience the promise of the Incarnation anew.

Day 27

Friday

'What then will this child become?'
Today's reading: Luke 1: 57–66

The miraculous birth of John forewarned Elizabeth, who seemed to understand much better than Zechariah, her husband, though he was the one who had had the vision, that Mary was to have an even greater cause for awe and wonder. Nevertheless, even this close to Christmas Day we should not forget the baby John, whose life was to be a blessing (that word again!) to Jesus as his ministry began to unfold. This Advent has brought us to the words of Isaiah many times, but now in Luke we hear the prophetic voice once more. The name 'John' indeed means 'blessed of God'. Is it the most perfect of names?

'What then will this child become?' is a question for all parents and, as one gets older, grandparents and aunts and uncles too. Many things we shall never know, and they pass into the mystery of God as they come from the mystery of God. But, and this is part of the wonder, the whole question is bound up in hope and love. We anticipate with joy; it bubbles up within us like the glow from an open fire on a freezing night or the surprise at finding a twenty pound or euro note that you had forgotten you had tucked in a book as a marker. The light of a star reaches the earth long after it was formed in a sun millions of miles away, but it falls on our eyes with a wonder that is both far and near, stretching the senses, holding us spell-bound, letting us dream and dream, walking in the night and embracing the dark, whilst hugging to our hearts the light of eternity.

The hours are few until the Nativity of our Lord, but the question is still about John. He remains to the end the enigma that stirs our minds to consider – Zechariah now certain – that this baby will be named for God, as the child of Mary will be named as Saviour. Slowly the day is dawning and the cries to awake out of sleep will be heard. Even as a child John the Baptist is preparing the way. Be attentive, consider, and let the tongue be loosed in blessing; for the hand of the Lord was with him.

In the days of busyness that assault us in the run up to Christmas, let's try and make the time for the questions that bring a sense of tingling anticipation into every fibre of our being, smiling though our eyes, springing in our step, dancing with the music of the new life that is Christ in us. 'What then will this child become?' He will be like you and me: a miracle of God's creation – and the even greater wonder that is to come – just like the incarnate Son of God himself; human, with an ability to love placed there by the Father by whose will we have our very being.

Day 28

Christmas Eve

'Blessed be the Lord God of Israel, for he has looked favourably
on his people and redeemed them.'
Today's reading: Luke 1:68–79

Christmas Eve for so many people is the day of Christmas. Clergy,
choirs and organists, readers, sacristan and acolyte, and everyone from
the child with a lighted candle to the elderly, wrapped in rugs and
love, who make Christmas for us so special. And then we listen, or
so we should, for the sound of the angels in glory before the fright-
ened shepherds this night, and when the song of Zechariah proclaim-
ing the birth of the forerunner meets the hope of that message given
in the fields outside the City of David, we know that our Advent
journey from Isaiah to the Gospel of Luke is complete. It is a journey
of the mind but also of the heart, for this night our hopes are fulfilled and through doubt and darkness, misunderstanding and sin,
we kneel at the threshold of Christ's nativity.

Slowly, quietly it happens, creeping up through the busy day of
preparation. The day slips into night and the wakefulness of Advent
becomes the glory and splendour of the Christmas itself. The violet
of penitence is replaced by the white or gold of celebration and,
through the tiredness, the carols of Christmas that many of us have
sung for weeks in schools and institutions, heard in shopping centres
and other public places, become fresh once more; the words alive with

the coming of the son of David, the first-born of Mary and Joseph, the incarnate child of God.

In the afternoon at the crib service at St Mary's Church in Swanage, I shall read the story of the Nativity with perhaps two hundred children present with their parents and grandparents. We may have twenty shepherds and as many angels, but what is the real draw are the live animals. There is a pen in the church with lambs and calves and a donkey at the door. The child in heart is drawn in. We reach and touch the straw, the rough hair of a calf, the oily wool of a lamb. The animals are in a strange place, but then so are we. Our sense of smell and feel is heightened. We feel joy at all the happiness around us. Yet in all the activity there is also a profound peace. Then the Church empties and a team of helpers prepares for the Christmas Carol service little more than two hours later, before we are back for the Midnight Mass – the Eucharist of the Nativity.

Let me take you to Christmas night many years ago, to my childhood in St Andrew's Hornchurch in Essex. It is well after midnight; the communion has ended but the songs of Christmas night are still ringing in my ears. My eyes are stinging with tiredness and running with tears in the cold air. I wearily mount my bike and cycle for home as a sung-out chorister in another age. It was a short ride. I could do it in my sleep, even now, and I was close to it then. And my thoughts? Well of bed and presents and a short night and little sleep, of family meals and crackers and sweets and all the things that boys just longed for at a time like this, but what lives to this day is a sense that, on this night above all nights, we had been part of a thin – wafer thin – brush with eternity; shared across the ages of human life and held in the heart of God. His love perfects all things in the miracle of the birth of his Son to Mary this night.

CHRISTMAS

Day 29

Christmas Day

'This will be a sign for you: you will find a child wrapped in
bands of cloth and lying in a manger.'
Today's reading: Luke 2:1–20

On Christmas Day, universally, the gospel readings are just two: either
the whole or part of the verses from Luke we are reading today or the
prologue to John's Gospel. Familiarity is essential for Christmas
services in churches throughout the land, especially when it comes
to the carols. You can hear the clergy say, 'We will have "O come all
ye faithful" because this is the only day on which to really sing out
the last verse, Yea Lord we greet thee, born this happy morning.'
Amongst more adventurous congregations the old hymn, 'Christians
awake, salute the happy morn ...', might be slipped in, but on the
whole it will be the common favourites; and why not?

Advent is over, the wait and the penitence has been completed and
Christmas is here. Well, maybe. The reality for lots of us is that Christmas has been celebrated for some weeks in the offices and schools, the
residential home and community centre, the restaurants and pubs, and
yes, the churches and parish halls all over these islands and beyond.
Christmas has developed over decades of commercialisation. The
increased leisure time and financial resources of some mean that is a
month-long celebration. Charities and institutions work hard to make
sure that those who are destitute or in ill-health, including the homeless and elderly, are not forgotten.

If one needs to see a reason for this then it is not hard to find. Sermons, homilies, addresses, talks, call them what you will, in churches today will remind us of a few salient things: the birth of a child taking place in a stable, away from home, to a couple who have been travelling and who have struggled to find a place to spend the night. It is happening amidst the animals; the dirt and smell and darkness may well be emphasised. In the fields there are people working through the night; shepherds tending their flocks. They are the ones given the sign and the vision of angels that announced it. This is God in his glory and majesty and power becoming human in normality, which means everything that we have got going on in our lives today. This is not an idealised birth, amongst all the comfort and support that can be provided, but it is perfect, because it is real. It is full of wonder; and the awe that the shepherds experienced we too may find, if we will look afresh at the scene in our mind's eye.

It is not that this is particularly pretty, though we do our best to make it such from Christmas card to Nativity play, but it is normal. That normality is the transforming moment for me in this account, and why today I shall rejoice in happiness and gratitude, and sing the most familiar of songs with the angels of heaven and everyone who lives in the greater light of Christ's nearer presence; today in the most miraculous and glorious way, Jesus was born on earth, and today he is re-born in our hearts as the most natural thing, because God loves us. We have sung and heard carols throughout Advent, but today it becomes fresh and new again as the message of the Incarnation, God with us, is realised once more.

Day 30

26 December: St Stephen's Day

'But filled with the Holy Spirit, he gazed into heaven and saw
the glory of God and Jesus standing at the right hand of God.'
Today's reading: Acts 7:51–60

This day, across Ireland, is always 'St Stephen's Day', whilst in
England, where I was born and brought up, it is always 'Boxing
Day'. This is one thing, amongst others, for which I am so grateful
to the Irish people: reminding us that the day after Christmas Day is
indeed a saint's day; and what a saint! Stephen, the first Christian
martyr, is, rightly, primarily remembered for the way in which he
died, forgiving his murderers on the pattern of Jesus himself at Calvary, but Stephen should also be remembered for the way he lived,
and the vision for which he too is noted.

As we arrive on the Luas (Dublin's tram), travelling from the south of
the city to its centre, the names of the stations are announced in Irish
and English. The terminus is 'St Stephen's Green', and the saint gets his
full title; we pull up at the stop, tumble out on to the narrow boarding
platforms often crowded with new travellers heading for Dundrum
and other suburbs of south Dublin. The Green is a well-maintained
and valuable lung for the workers in the busy shops and offices of
the area, not to mention those passing by as tourists or commuters.

Yet there is more, for the gardens are maintained to a high stan-
dard and lovingly tended by individuals with hoe and sprinkler. There

is a glory to the formal bed of colourful planting varying, as with other parks and gardens, according to the season of the year. It is always the same but always different in another sense. So it is with the followers of Christ, and especially those who met at the stable; the shepherds of last night, and, if they did in fact appear before Mary and Joseph moved elsewhere, the wise men too, as they arrived some time later. They understood, if we read the Scriptures correctly, that the birth of Jesus was something miraculous and in the order of God's providence. It had been foretold by the prophets and expected for many years.

Stephen too was transfixed with the glory of God and the presence of Jesus interceding for him. It is a similar thing that we can experience as the heightening of the awareness of the miracle of the Incarnation brings us to contemplate the mystery with which God, in his love, brought this to be. People tumbling into and out of trains and buses and trams are nearly all repeating the same journey along the same rails or road each day; yet occasionally, and maybe not very often, everyone is stopped and brought up to experience an old path with fresh eyes. Perhaps as we run down the Luas stops to the end: '… Ranelagh, Harcourt, St Stephen's Green' we might just spare a thought for the man who died and gave his name both to this day and to the gardens in which I have eaten many an M & S sandwich. A meal deal that includes the park bench, the flowers, the gaily dressed Dubliners of all nations, all washed down with an inner yearning to know how it is that one so visionary as Stephen seemed such a threat to those who too sought the face of the living God. Maybe the stable would have been a better place to meet.

Day 31

27 December: St John the Evangelist's Day

'If it is my will that he remain until I come,
what is that to you?'
Today's reading: John 21:19b–25

It does seem strange that the three days after Christmas Day all relate to death rather than birth. Yet Peter's reference to John in these verses receives a comment from Jesus indicating that the beloved disciple may not die, or at least not yet. In the coming days we shall be reading from the First Epistle of John. This is a text that relates us constantly back to the nature of God being of the nature of love, and the call to the abiding in love will occur again and again.

In John's Gospel there is a deeply theological and spiritual undergirding to all that is being related to us by the Evangelist. The John who is the author of the Fourth Gospel, if identified as he traditionally is with the Apostle John, was a fisherman like Simon, Andrew and James, but imagine what mystery of inner development has taken place. John has lived this through a transformation with Christ from his first call from the fishing nets in Galilee to the end of a long life. This is the thought that we grasp, of his giving of himself, as he tells the story of the life of Jesus in his Gospel.

John doesn't begin with the birth of Jesus. That story is in the accounts by Luke and Matthew. However, he does say amazing things in his prologue about the incarnation and the coming of the

'Word'. At Christmas we relate spiritually and emotionally to the majestic opening verses of John's Gospel, partially, I suggest, because they *are* majestic, and have the ring of authority, partially because they aid us in unpicking the truth of the Incarnation in words that speak to our hearts of the things of Christmas: light and life, the coming of John the Baptist, and the preparation and the expectation that accompany the confounding of the sin and darkness of this fallen world.

So it is that John's long life led him to be able to reflect much on the earlier days of Christ's physical appearance on this earth as an infant, a boy and a man. We look to Bethlehem today, even though our reading is from Galilee. Why? Because that is where our hearts and minds rest over these days of Christmas: the wise men still travelling, the shepherds still in the Nativity stable, though long since having gone back to their field rejoicing; the picture is etched there somewhere for us to create in imagination, whilst holding the truth of the birth of Jesus closely to our hearts.

I expect the actual sales in shops are getting going now and the tills ringing with the returns and Christmas vouchers too, though online there will have been many transactions already. My father-in-law used to say, either today, or even yesterday, 'Christmas is as far away as ever now' meaning that it is past and the next one is a year away. He loved a family Christmas and some years ago, towards the end of his life, he managed with oxygen and long day-time naps to share with us once more the love of family celebrating the love of God.

Many of us know that love shared in the midst with those who are no longer physically with us, but in the words of the traditional bidding prayer for the King's College Nine Lessons and Carols, 'rejoice on a farther shore and in a greater light'. For our children, all four grandparents have now passed into that new life and eternal light and presence to which our liturgy, in unity, brings us near. This day is indeed about birth as well as about death; more importantly it is about love and abiding, watchfulness in the eternal sense of seeking ever to be with Christ, and the humility to glimpse in the Christ-child the confirmation of all our hopes.

Day 32

28 December: The Holy Innocents

'Get up, take the child and his mother, and flee to Egypt ...'
Today's reading: Matthew 2:13–18

For many years I served as a priest in a parish, and then in a cathedral, where the saints' days after Christmas are all duly observed. Very few people come to the Eucharist on these days; for most the time is passed in other pursuits, and the Holy Innocents are little thought of, unless the commemoration falls on a Sunday. As we read these verses from Matthew, we are now, in terms of the chronology of the Gospels, already post-Epiphany, which in the Church year we haven't reached yet. We are in the days after the coming of the Wise Men. It was their attention to detail and carefully calculated times that alerted Herod to the potential risk of a rival king. We manage by telescoping time for the Holy Innocents' Day to demonstrate the danger to Jesus and his parents in close proximity to the day of the birth, whilst it may have occurred perhaps two weeks later.

The escaping Holy Family we shall return to in a moment, but first let us dwell on the terrible slaying of the babies of Bethlehem. This unforgivable murder is hard to hold in the context of the birth stories of Jesus, yet it is a unique day that brings to our remembrance more than a little real life. The abuse of the vulnerable is most obvious and brutal, but next to this we have the jealousy and hard-edged fear of Herod and the callous and unquestioning violence of the soldiers. They, we may say, can have no more blame attached to them than the soldiers who nailed Jesus to the Cross, but in the cause of human dignity and compassion there is little else that can be justifiably said in their defence.

How does this fit the fourth day of Christmas when in popular Christmas celebration we are far from contemplating the horror of the murder of babies? The child is symbolic of Christmas. Parents will spend their last pounds and euros, their precious hours of sleep, much of their free time – not to mention hours of thought and planning – to ensure that their children have a happy Christmas. By this time there may be a few toys that have broken, batteries that have run out or even amongst the more over-indulged of youngsters a certain languid boredom that is looking already for the next thing to excite or entertain them.

But today we are not contemplating the ordinary attempts at comforting the well-off, we are bringing the injustice and cruelty of the world towards the weak and defenceless right into the homes of our church and community. In this country we know that the wealthy can, to a large extent, insulate themselves from the actions of the powerful, but the poor cannot. In Bethlehem there were families that could not simply leave home and flee, even given warning, of which there appeared to be none, but had to stay and suffer the consequences, as the vulnerable always do in situations from which they cannot escape.

Joseph and Mary were fortunate. Joseph received a message in a dream, and he knew that they must leave and travel to Egypt, where they remained for some time. This is a long way, which would take hours by coach or car and weeks on foot. But they were safe, and bided their time until the threat to Jesus was much reduced. Again, the providence of God is revealed in these verses from Matthew.

In Cairo there are beautiful Coptic churches that are dedicated to this sojourn by the Holy Family in a foreign land, in the land of the

Exodus. In the course of this century, of which we are now in its third decade, the plight of fleeing peoples has never gone away. Many have survived extreme trauma and have made a new life; many others have perished in the attempt. Let this day be a day to remember the lost and the suffering of the helpless.

Day 33

29 December: The Fifth Day of Christmas

'... the inner thoughts of many will be revealed ...'
Today's reading: Luke 2:22–35

Caught up in celebrations, it is easy to forget just how quickly the days of Christmas slip by, and when looked at from this distance, run into one another. By this the fifth day of Christmas some people have returned to work, children will already be thinking about going back to school and older students could be starting to consider doing some study. The New Year looms with fireworks and resolutions, but within a few days we are back to normal, and we forget that the Christmas and Epiphany period extends some distance yet – right up to 2 February: the Presentation of Christ in the Temple, or Candlemas, for short. Today and tomorrow we anticipate that festival by reading the gospel accounts of the two main figures: Simeon and Anna.

Simeon, whom we encounter today, is one of the great ponderers of the Bible. He sat looking and listening day by day. He understood the human heart and had a visionary sight of what was to come too, for individuals at least. He knew also when he had encountered the Christ. His song, known to us as the '*Nunc Dimittis*', has become one of the most frequently used canticles in the Christian Church: part of Evensong, part of Compline, read at funerals by priests as an act of commendation, read by individuals in their night-time prayers, pondered on as light of one sort or another passes away.

Recently, I heard a preacher start her address with the interesting fact (which she confessed to have found on the internet) that the word 'silent' has the same letters as the word 'listen'. Although Simeon was recorded as speaking by Luke, whilst Anna was not, his days in the Temple must have held a great deal of inner silence and contemplative listening, which as the letters in a different order incidentally show us are related to one another, and to such other qualities as stillness and patience. These we cultivate or not, as our days of Christmas may show only too well. Desire for them and our capacity to fulfil them may depend significantly upon how we live our lives, and the demands upon them, but, it has to be said that we do not necessarily use space wisely even when we have it.

The context of Simeon's waiting is bound with a certain state of assurance. That is what Simeon feels, and it is reflected in his words. He has 'seen the salvation of our God', that is enough. Many of us have witnessed elderly relations and friends that are living already in a closer consciousness of the presence of Christ than those of us more active and busy. They spend their days sitting quietly in prayerful silence, disturbed by meals and the conversation of visitors; but their inner life, the revelation of their heart, is already in Christ in a special way. Simeon, and Anna, whom we shall meet tomorrow, were both on that higher spiritual plane, and they would, no doubt, see in a way that embraced the humility of God, as further and completely revealed in the Christ-child.

Day 34

30 December: The Sixth Day of Christmas

'At that moment she came and began to praise God ...'
Today's reading: Luke 2: 36–40

Simeon we thought of yesterday, in silence and in speech, but what of Anna, the second person in the Temple to be drawn to the baby Jesus? She hasn't left us with words as Simeon has, but by the way that Luke describes her, she is like many devout women in every age and every place, whose life revolves around the sacred place of worship, with fasting and prayer night and day. She too is a waiter and watcher; someone for whom God, and redemption, and vision, are her life. She is described as a prophetess, and Luke seems to indicate that she is somehow led to be present at that 'very hour' when Christ would appear.

From these two elderly people it can be seen how the Church sees the Feast of the Presentation of Christ in the Temple (falling as it does at the beginning of February) as being the point between Christmas and Easter at which our attention is being directed onwards to the cross. Yet it comes with a feeling of completion, both from Simeon and from Anna. A long vigil is over, and they recognise that what they have been looking for has come. They both see it, or better: they both see Christ in the infant Jesus. That watershed of Candlemas we can understand better on 2 February than where we are today, on 30 December, heading into the eve of the New Year tomorrow. Anna, as a person of prophetic insight, causes us to reflect on this day as well; for insight into how things are in the present moment is an important part of the turning of the year, and inclination and foresight to be in the right place at the right time is also a prophetic gift – and one that many of us would dearly like to have!

Simeon and Anna are amongst the most attractive figures in the New Testament, for they demonstrate more than a few of the core virtues for which Christians strive: patience, hope, vision, self-effacement, trust, discipline, conviction, persistence and, ultimately, confirmation of the presence of our Lord, revealed in awe and wonder. Simeon and Anna were fulfilled in their search and encouraged by the gift to them of the sight of their salvation.

The path ahead was clear for Anna as it was for Simeon, in so far as they were filled with hope. The destination, we know, with the advantage of being 2000 years beyond the Cross and Resurrection of Christ, but our response is new every morning; so we become the watchers and waiters like Anna and Simeon and are renewed with their hope and vision.

Day 35

31 December: The Seventh Day of Christmas

'And I myself have seen and have testified that
this is the Chosen One.'
Today's reading: John 1:29–34

John the Baptist was as sure as anyone can be of his role in the preparation of the way for the Messiah. The conviction with which we read his words, and hear his testimony, is a tonic for all of us whose steps are in the frail and insecure path of questioning whilst life is throwing all sorts of problems our way, which for most of us is some time or other.

Today is called either New Year's Eve or Old Year's Night and one that for most people is celebratory. For some, at least, it is a moment of real reflection on how things have been over the past twelve months, and perhaps a time to form resolutions, looking forward positively and in hope, no matter what the outcome of the year that has gone has been. John the Baptist is a particularly strong individual and few if any of us have his unshakable conviction, but, laying that aside for a moment, let us consider what John the Evangelist is recording of his namesake's words. Today's gospel reading is almost entirely composed of John the Baptist's proclamation about Christ. He speaks of himself in relation to our Lord, and they were related both in their calling, as they were in their family ties.

John concludes, on the basis of his experience at the baptism of Jesus, that his cousin was the 'Son of God'. What exactly he meant by that may be the subject of discussion, as we cannot simply place our developed theological understanding of the person of Christ on John's exclamation of wonder. However, the earlier words of John in this passage suggest that he saw in Jesus, the Messiah; the one who is to redeem the people.

Building upon our thoughts from Simeon and Anna in the past two days, we conclude the year in the company of these visionary servants of God with something of their hope and expectation, and that we may also feel on the eve of something new and hopeful. As midnight approaches so the anticipation is ignited and memories stirred. A few years ago now, on a special Old Year's Night, my wife and I were phoned, on the stroke of midnight, by our son to say he and his girlfriend were engaged to be married, and that set all our thoughts in a new way as the New Year dawned. Such can be the effect of a few words with a deep and lasting significance, and such are John's reflections on the appearance of the Saviour.

Day 36

1 January: The Naming and Circumcision of Jesus

'When the eighth day came, it was time to circumcise the child,
and he was called Jesus ...'
Today's reading: Luke 2:15–21

The writer Ronald Blythe, best known for his book *Akenfield*, first published in 1969 and a classic description of English village life, but author of many books, and weekly contributor to the *Church Times* for a score or more years, had a habit on 1 January of seeing how many different flowers were blooming in his garden on that day. He suggested that the observant will conclude, 'a surprisingly large number'. I expect that most families and individuals have their own New Year festive traditions. The hardy may wild swim, probably as part of an organised event raising money or just for fun, splashing enthusiastically into freezing cold water, especially at the seaside. Photographs in the newspapers the next day will show crowds rushing down a beach in wetsuits, swimming costumes and fancy dress and diving into the water. Walks and sporting events may occupy us too, though there is lying in bed also, especially for those who have celebrated the passing of the old year and seeing in the new in a way that demanded the stamina to keep up with those full of the party spirit.

Even amongst regular churchgoers today few will note that this is the eighth day of Christmas. 1 January is known in the Church calendar as the Festival of the Circumcision or the 'Naming of Jesus'. This is set on this day as in Luke 2:21, we read, 'When the eighth day came, it was time to circumcise the child, and he was called Jesus'. So, it isn't actually anything to do with the fact that it is the beginning of a new calendar year, but, somehow, I think that that is what will be uppermost in people's minds today. A New Year, a new opportunity – a new hope.

Opportunity and hope are two words that can ring hollow in the hearts of those who have little prospect of either due to the condition of their life. This is surely where the modern celebration of the New Year, marking a parting of the ways, and the old Church tradition of drawing attention to Christ's dedication in name and the indelible placing of him physically within his religious tradition, meet. The baby Jesus was a real hope for his family and for his people as has been expressed by prophet and seer not only in the preceding generations, but even as we have noted in the last three days in these reflections, in the hearts and minds of those living in his day. It was an indefinable hope. It was a hope that God was to bring to humanity a sewing up of the unravelling of the perfection of Creation. The reality was that the community of which Jesus was a part was helpless to better its situation. Help must come from beyond it. The birth of Jesus was not only the promise of that help, he was also to be the agent of its fulfilment.

If we place this parallel with the condition of those who cannot help themselves in today's world, the desire of those people who can transform lives is injected with energy today. We can fulfil what it is within our power to do and bring change for good to those who look for hope from beyond themselves – and believe that it will come.

Day 37

2 January: The Ninth Day of Christmas

'They said to him, "Who are you?"'
Today's reading: John 1: 19–28

Priests and Levites came from Jerusalem to John the Baptist, who was baptising at a place known as Bethany beyond the Jordan, which was close to Jericho. They were sent by the authorities to clarify what they had been hearing. 'Who are you?', has ever been, and ever will be, a question for each of us to address, and in a wider interpretation is a crucial identity issue of our day. Living for much of my adult life in and around Belfast, culture, religion, history, language and ethnicity are things that are impossible to ignore. One might say that the Jewish authorities in John's day were being diligent in ascertaining his identity directly from his mouth. How easy it is to work on preconceived ideas and stereotypes and neatly file individuals and communities. To some extent at least we all do it.

John, it has been assumed, was, or had been, a member of an ascetic sect, possibly at the nearby settlement of Qumran. His outlook and teaching would confirm us in this opinion and explain why he chose the nearest point of constant fresh running water to offer baptism to those who came seeking it.

The ninth day of Christmas and the matter of how we identify ourselves are presented to us by today's reading. Can we indeed be allowed to say who we are? Are there things about who we are that we cannot deny or wish away? Yes, of course there are. But the unseen, the things that we process in head and heart that cause us to identify in a particular way, are critical, and surely this was what the priests and Levites were sent to extract from John, rather than his family background or more immediate past history.

The sensitivity of the question, 'Who are you?' is not insignificant either. It may be interpreted in a judgemental way. We want to know in order that we can neatly compartmentalise you as a person. In a way, this is also relevant to John the Baptist, as to whether or not he could be considered a real threat or simply a passing annoyance. In the 2020s the question is more likely to be considered rude, as its directness should be hedged with the genuinely offered freedom not to answer, unless it is a formal requirement, for example in an application for admission to something or somewhere.

Directed to ourselves, as an individual, beginning-of-the-year look at our lifestyle, we may quickly dismiss the question as something to consider carefully and deeply *when we have the time*. This is what most of us do; we deliberately avoid the kind of navel gazing that is unhelpful, but the ultimate questions of life are bound up with these three simple words, 'Who are you?' The beginning of the year may be a time for this question, but more likely we consider it at one of life's great events: serious illness, bereavement, moving house, marriage, childbirth, retirement. At these times a moment for reassessing things is inevitable. Being comfortable with who we are is one of the great secrets of life, and whether on this day we pass quickly over the question to John or take it to our own heart to answer probably rests on how we have addressed it in the past.

Day 38

'Child, why have you treated us like this?'
Today's reading: Luke 2:41–52

The reading before us today only appears once in three years in the Sunday Eucharistic lectionary (on the Sunday after Christmas in Year C). I have a feeling that this may have been debated by the liturgists at length as the rest of the chapter is read every year, and this is, after all, the only account we have in the canonical Gospels relating to the boyhood of Jesus.

We lost our son in a large store in Belfast when he was quite small. Children can disappear amongst racks of clothing or round the corner of an aisle in a supermarket in a few seconds. It is one of the nightmares of parenthood, and it has happened to plenty of us. Mostly it ends up alright in the end, and our son was found curled up asleep in the window, amongst the display. But let us draw back from our own anxieties and consider what has happened to Mary and Joseph to cause Jesus' mother to declare, 'Child, why have you treated us like this?'

There is so little information available to help us build a picture of the childhood of Jesus, and we can but speculate on how his spiritual development was revealed through word and deed to his parents and friends. However what is revealed in the reading before us today is that at the age of twelve he was contemplating his place as a child of

God in a way beyond what he heard and understood from those closest to him in Nazareth. He was being drawn to know more of the expectations and vision of one whose spiritual apprehension had already brought him to feel God intimately and as close as a Father to him.

How we bring our inner feelings to bear upon the considerations of others is a subject for on-going reflection, but Jesus sought to know more through any pathway and an obvious one to him was to take the opportunity of his time in the Temple. Physically impressive, the building also reflected the seriousness of the people who created it and those who continued to pray within its walls around the need for service to God who is at the centre of all things.

Many people consider our day to be one of religious crisis, conflict and deep consideration of past failings. Some look upon our church buildings as irrelevant or reflective of a time long gone. Others see them as reminders that Christianity in reforming itself for a new age must be careful not to remove the very houses of God that can be the same centres of learning, sanctuary, inspiration and beauty that they have ever been.

For all the faults of the Temple and those who taught in it, Jesus recognised it for what it was; he was seeking more than something symbolic. Our Lord, as a child of twelve, was asking questions; he knew what he wanted to understand more fully and was singleminded to the point of forgetting to let his parents in on the secret. The answer to Mary's question is simple, and Jesus saw that it should have been obvious to those who were closest to him: 'Did you not know that I must be in my Father's house?' Thus the incident is concluded but not closed. Jesus' mother, like all mothers who are coming to understand their children better, 'treasured all these things in her heart'.

Day 39

4 January: The Eleventh Day of Christmas

'What are you looking for?'
Today's reading: John 1:35–42

All manner of professional people, from teachers and priests to doctors, nurses and politicians, and even those involved in finance and lifestyle, are quite used to teasing out the real reason why they are being consulted by someone. Ostensibly problems or decisions are presented in a way that seems sensible, but the experinced individual offering counsel can sense that this is not the only or even the most important issue. Human beings are adept at masking what is really going on, and the vital ingredient in someone's personal concern may not reveal itself directly, or if it does, it is as they are closing the door on leaving.

'Journeying to the Light' is the title I settled on for this book after trying many alternatives. Trying to sum up what I was attempting in writing started with a daily marking of the way to Christmas, but leading right on to the Epiphany begged the question, put to me by wife, 'How do you deal with the climax coming part way through and not at the end, as with a Lent book? 'What are you looking for?' is such a good question for so many situations in which we find ourselves. The disciples of John, who are asked this question by Jesus, give a slightly enigmatic answer: 'Rabbi, where are you staying?' On the one had it suggests that if they were leaving our Lord's consulting room and were tackled with a repeat of the question, they would answer, as the door swung closed, 'You'. On the other hand, it may mean, 'We don't know, but want to ask you about it.' In other words, having listened to John, they felt a growing clarity of vision and hope for the future but needed to know more. They sought light for the path.

The climax of the Epiphany was not going to exceed that of the Nativity, but it did crystallise the essential message that the baby Jesus was God incarnate and his place as Saviour and King was open for proclamation. With that announcement the effects were instant and obvious: the bowing of the nations to the new-born king amongst those who looked for his coming, and the panicked reaction of those who opposed this miraculous and eternal change to the order of God's involvement in his creation. Light was coming, and indeed had already arrived, in the midst of the darkness of human failure and sin. The light that in the Epiphany shone forth from the birthplace of the Christ-child is the light that lightens the heart of all of us whose seeking, whether we know it or not, is for a deeper understanding of what that life is all about. What we in our day discover is that love's consequences are challenging in the extreme, but the infinite possibilities of exploring the love of God for each of us bring us to a new place on the journey of life that is unaccountably wonderful, for all its demands upon us.

Day 40

5 January: The Twelfth day of Christmas

'Where did you get to know me?'
Today's reading: John 1:43–51

The last day of Christmas and the eve of the Epiphany and we encounter Nathaniel's question to Jesus. With the level of personal data sharing that there is today, even with the legislation protecting us against information misuse, we may be surprised to discover how someone has been able to trace us, or know us on social media, though it's more with the thought, 'How did they manage that?', than with any genuine sense of shock that some person or organisation has managed it.

How did the Wise Men manage to meet together and work out the times and expectations that they shared? How did John the Baptist know when was the moment to announce the arrival of the Lamb of God? How did Jesus know that the fishermen would leave their nets and follow him? How did Nathaniel come to be known by our Lord? There is a discovery that all who are called by Christ come to make. It is simply that it has happened at all. How have I come to be known? This is part of the mysterious working of God with humanity, that we can be loved as individuals in the midst of the billions of our fellow creatures.

As the hours tick on towards the proclamation that is the Epiphany tomorrow, so the deep realisation that what is common to all is specific to me – and you – cannot but be received with a joy that is infectious and inspirational. What we have others too may possess. How we are known is also how others are known.

Maybe there is another lesson for us in this? We acknowledge that, as far as our place in the scale of human existence is concerned, we are less than a grain of sand on the seashore, but are we not also drawn to the microscopic? The structure of life is fascinating in its intricacy and unimaginable textures and cellular complexities are revealed the closer we look. Not that we are playing God, but we are apprehending the structure and design of God's creation on a scale that we would not ordinarily contemplate. Let us marvel at how we are known, and at the same time seek to see more deeply what is all around us.

Day 41

6 January: The Epiphany

'... they offered him gifts of gold and frankincense and myrrh.'
Today's reading: Matthew 2:1–12

Epiphany is remembered as the first public showing of the Christ-child. Orthodox Church paintings traditionally show Mary holding out the baby for the adoration of the wise men. These strangers had travelled great distances to worship the child and bring their gifts. This is the time foretold by the prophets, when the ends of the earth would bow down to the king. In Jesus Christ the kingdom of God has come amongst us.

In many of the traditional Christmas carols, the Son of God is described as having 'come down', stooping low, descending – thus 'to come from highest bliss, down to such a world as this'. The impression that we are expected to be left with is one of humility and lowliness, but that Christ arrived at that state from highest heaven. This is, of course, using the imagery of the three-fold universe, with heaven above us and hell below us; though we no longer use this description of the universe physically and technically, it continues to hold a picture that is both easy to understand and reflects the actual truth – albeit in an old-fashioned way. The images of God stooping low to bless us and of Christ coming down from a lofty throne to share our life and die for us are images that we find to be remarkably meaningful, even though they reflect an outdated picture of the universe. Power we associate with height, weakness with the ground, kneeling, bowing, prostrating; we cannot defend ourselves adequately while lying on the ground; we are at the mercy of someone standing over us.

Today as the wise men approach the infant Jesus, it is noteworthy to remind ourselves that these men knelt and paid the Christ-child homage. They did not just come in and, standing in the stable, talk to Mary and Joseph, saying, and by the way we have some presents for the baby, and we know that he is to be a great king. This is not an act of kindness, or generosity, or even the gift of a well-wisher. These are the gifts of someone paying homage – here we see grown men kneel. Nor is it a little bow, this is prostration, adoration, homage.

They were honest, open men too: honest with Herod, thus exposing the one they had come to see to danger. The whole situation ends in turmoil, as the wise men find a different route home, Mary, Joseph and Jesus flee to Egypt, and Herod attempts to destroy this threat to his kingdom. But the story continues as a parable to its end; the teaching of the parable being that the light of Christ will not be hidden. It is the message of the Epiphany too, that what is revealed to the wise men has changed forever power and authority on earth; they saw it, were prostrate and worshipped, for Christ was more than a baby in a stable but showed forth the love and humility of God for all time and for all peoples.

The Epiphany is a reminder to us today that things are not always what they seem, and that in the eyes of faith and wonder and wisdom and love, even in deepest darkness a light is shining; for Christ is unchanging, and God is unchanging, and our eternal hope lies where it did for the wise men, in what is true and eternal and wonderful, even the person of Christ himself, who for our sakes became poor so that we, through his poverty, might become rich.